# GOLF
## THE EARLY DAYS

19.—CHARLES I.
A Royal and Ancient Golfer.

# GOLF
## THE EARLY DAYS

ROYAL & ANCIENT GAME
FROM ITS ORIGINS TO 1939

DALE CONCANNON

SMITHMARK

A Salamander Book

This edition published in 1995 by SMITHMARK Publishers Inc.
16 East 32nd Street, New York, NY 10016

1 3 5 7 9 8 6 4 2

ISBN 0 8317 5513 X

SMITHMARK books are available for bulk purchase for sales
promotion and premium use. For details write or call the manager
of special sales, SMITHMARK Publishers Inc, 16 East 32nd Street,
New York, NY 10016 ; (212) 532-6600

All correspondence concerning the content of this book should
be addressed to Salamander Books Ltd,
129–137 York Way, London N7 9LG, England

Credits
Editor : Krystyna Zukowska
Designer : John Clark, BA (Hons)
Photographer : Elizabeth Jane McNulty
Produced for Salamander by
The Book Package Co. Ltd, Bournemouth, England
Page make-up : Image Design, Christchurch, England
Color Reproduction by Appletone Graphics, Bournemouth, England
Printed in Italy

## Acknowledgments

The author would like to express his grateful thanks to the auction houses of Phillips, Sotheby's and Christies for their help in providing photographs of golfing antiques. I would especially like to thank Bob G. Gowland, Director of Phillips (Chester) for his help in providing material for the photographic spreads. Thanks also to John A. Joinson, Phillips (Chester), Krystyna Zukowska and Richard Collins at Salamander Books, Peter Lewis, Curator of the British Golf Museum, St Andrews, Walter Mechilli of Moseley Golf Club, Michael and Margaret Hobbs and innumerable private golf collectors for their help and assistance. Finally, most special thanks to Christina Steinmann, without whose never-failing patience, encouragement and understanding this book would not have been written.

To my golfing Uncle, Terry Concannon.

Front and back endpapers: *Ladies playing golf on Minchinhampton Common. This painting by Lucien Davis, R.I., was commissioned by the* Illustrated London News *in 1890.*

Title page: *A stylized illustration of women playing golf at the turn of this century.*

# CONTENTS

*This drawing by Charles Crombie (1885–1967) was part of a series produced by the artist for Perrier of France in 1905. Each is a comic illustration of a rule of golf. Crombie worked for* Punch *and produced postcards and book illustrations.*

RULE I (§)
"Out of bounds"
is any place
outside the···
···· course ·

*'Golf on the Ice'. Painted in 1668 by Adriaen van de Velde (1636–1672), the scene depicts play near Haarlem, Holland.*

The exact origins of golf are unknown. Like some complex jigsaw puzzle with many of the key pieces missing, its early history remains vague and incomplete. Many theories have been put forward but none offers conclusive evidence where or when golf was first played or who originally played it.

Searching for the origins of golf in other early European games has been a favorite occupation of golf historians. Since Victorian times any 'stick and ball' game which bore even a fleeting similarity to golf has been examined for evidence of an early link. The fourteenth-century 'Crecy Window' in Gloucester Cathedral shows someone about to strike a ball with a club but whether this is golf or some other ancient pastime has long been open to debate. Most recently, a German writer called Herbert Riedal maintained that golf was first played in China over a thousand years ago. Other equally serious claims to be the birthplace of golf have come from France, Italy, Holland and even Japan.

Although Scotland is widely credited with being the home of golf, its claim, like many others, is based on tradition rather than hard historical fact. The first reference to golf came in 1457, when King James II of Scotland proclaimed that, 'fute-baw and golf be uterly cryt done and not usyt...'. With England threatening invasion from the south, the King expressed concern that the popularity of both sports were actively interfering with

Left: *A 'golfer' depicted in the Great East Window of Gloucester Cathedral.*
Above: *A selection of lofted mallets and wooden balls used in the ancient French game of Jue de Mail. Known as Pall Mall in England, the ball was lobbed through a series of hoops, croquet style, with the finishing hoop being described as a 'passe'.*

his subjects' archery practice. With trained archers vital to the defence of his realm, daily practice was already compulsory for every Scottish male aged twelve or over. Consequently, the playing of golf and football were outlawed and banned in Scotland for the next sixty years.

Historically, this edict shows how popular and widespread golf must have been in fifteenth century Scotland but offers little clue as to how the game actually started. So the question remains: how did golf begin? The root idea of the game, that of striking a ball to any given point in as few strokes as possible, is common to many ancient civilizations. As early as in Roman times, a sport called *paganica* was popular with the common soldiery. Played with a 'bent stick,' it involved hitting a leather ball stuffed with feathers across open land towards a target like a tree stump or well. Thought to have been introduced into Britain during the Roman occupation of the first century, the game has long been considered a possible forerunner of golf. While no evidence exists that *paganica* survived the departure of the Romans in the third century, the actual leather ball is remarkably similar to the 'feathery' used in the early years of Scottish golf.

Another early pastime linked with the origins of golf if the fourteenth century English game of *cambucca* or *cambuc*. Popular during the reign of Edward III, *cambuc* differed from the Roman game of *paganica* in that a wooden ball was used rather than a leather one. Played across open countryside, a *baculus incurvatus* or curved club was used to propel the ball forward. The possibility that *cambuc* was some sort of missing-link between the ancient Roman game and early golf has always been hotly debated. Written records of the period do, however, throw up a curious coincidence. In a proclamation issued by King Edward III to all Sheriffs of England in 1363, it stated that:

'Every able-bodied man on feast days when he has leisure,
shall in his sports use bows and arrows, pellets and bolts,
and shall learthe practice and art of shooting. Forbidding
all and  singular on pain of imprisonment, football, club-
ball, *cambuc,* cock-fighting and other vain games.'

Right: *A form of indoor golf was played centuries ago by the Japanese. Here, two Japanese women are seen playing the game in kimonos.*

Left: *Thought to have been used from the sixteenth century onwards, this club with its elaborate crested design, dates from the first quarter of the eighteenth century.*

Of course this highly speculative link proves nothing. Golf well may have been thriving in Scotland long before 1457, with *cambuc* nothing more than an exclusively English pastime. The use of a wooden ball would also seem to rule out any link with golf, except there is the possibility that golf was not only played with feather balls, but with a more common wooden version also. In 1614, the Earl of Caithness described a siege at Kirkwall thus: 'The walls were strong, the canon balls of the besiegers were broken like golf balls and cloven in two halves.'

Feather balls made from stitched leather would not break in two but would rather split at the seams, and most golfing scholars take this to mean that wooden balls were used in the original game. However, in the search for possible early links with golf, it would be a mistake to assume the game we enjoy today is the same one which was played over five centuries ago. The game of golf, like other ancient sports, has evolved through the centuries to fit the needs of those who played it.

Another sport which used a wooden ball was the ancient French game of *jeu de mail*. Originally played in the open coun-

tryside, the course was usually a track or tree-lined road. Unlike previous pastimes, *jeu de mail* was played within strict boundaries, with penalties for those who left the 'fairway'. For example, if the ball left the road the player was penalized three hits or strokes (it has been suggested that this was the origin of the out of bounds rule.) So strong was this claim in Victorian times that a description of it was published in *Historical Gossip about Golf and Golfers* in 1863:

'The goals (targets) are not very long, averaging perhaps half a mile. At the end of each is placed a touchstone, as it is called, which the players have to strike before the match is won, and he who can do it in the least number of strokes, wins.'

The wooden-shafted hammer (or mallet) used to hit the ball was designed with a lofted striking face similar to an early golf club. Introduced into England in the first quarter of the seventeenth century, Charles I was a devotee from his early years in France, and was instrumental in developing the first courses in London. Known as *pall mall* in England, it was originally played along some of the quieter avenues in the capital. Then as life in London gradually became more crowded and less safe, it evolved into a far more sedate game played inside enclosed courts.

Favored by fashionable London society, the ball was lobbed through a series of metal hoops more akin to croquet than golf. Before dying out in the late eighteenth century, the site of one of London's earliest courses left its permanent mark on the city in the form of a street name; the tree-lined avenue leading up to Buckingham Palace along which Charles II is thought to have played is called to this day Pall Mall.

Like other theories, much of this evidence is circumstantial. Early illustrations show the ball was hit side on like golf, but the game in Scotland had already been in existence centuries before Charles I ever came to the English throne. Indeed over a century before, Mary, Queen of Scots, was known to have played both golf and pall mall. This does suggest that if the

Left: *This illustration from* Nouvelles Regles pour le Jeu de Mail, *published in 1717, clearly shows the similarity between the swing used in golf and the ancient French game of Jeu de Mail (Pall Mall). Known to have been played by Charles I, it was introduced into England in the early seventeenth century.*

mere act of hitting a ball with a stick is seen as evidence the game's origins will never be settled.

In recent years, the strongest challenge to Scotland comes from Holland and the game of *kolf*. This Dutch theory gained recognition in 1972, when renowned golf historians Steven Van Hengel published his ground-breaking book, *Early Golf*. Having extensively researched the Dutch archives, he showed that an early version of golf was played in Holland as early as the thirteenth century – well over 150 years before it was recorded as being played in Scotland.

According to Van Hengel, golf evolved from the ancient Dutch game of *spel metten kolve*, later shortened to *het kolve*, then finally to *kolf*. Deriving much of his information from the city ordinances designed to protect the public from the errant shots of early players, he traced this golf-like game back to Boxing Day 1297. He discovered that in Loenan aan de Vecht, a small town south of Utrecht, townspeople commemorated the relief of Kronenburg Castle by playing *kolf* on the local four-hole course. With holes measuring over one thousand yards apart, it is slightly misleading to use the term a 'four-hole course'. The term 'hole' is also questionable, when in reality the targets were four doors – on a windmill, a kitchen, a courthouse, and the castle itself.

Little is known about how the game was played or what rules, if any, there were. It was thought to have been played in the open countryside until the early seventeenth century, where a sudden increase in popularity brought eager Dutch *kolfers* into the town's squares and streets. Then just as suddenly, owing to the damage caused to property and concern for public safety, it returned once more to the open countryside.

Often depicted as a winter pastime, *kolf* was also played over the frozen lakes and canals of ·Holland. It was thought there were no holes as such in *kolf*, only a series of ornately

Above: 'Golf on the Ice' by Hendrik Avercamp (1585–1634). Played over the frozen rivers and canals of lowland Holland, Dutch 'Kolf' is thought to be a forerunner of early golf. Played to a marker or post frozen into the ice, it was supposedly introduced into Scotland by Flemish merchants in the fifteenth century, where it gradually evolved into the game we have today.

carved posts in winter and targets like those at Loenan in summer. However, in 1861 the British Museum purchased an early sixteenth-century Flemish manuscript entitled the *Book of Hours* which supposedly proved otherwise. At the base of one page, a painted miniature by artist Simon Bennink clearly shows a group of four players standing around a hole, with one kneeling down ready to tap in. This early representation is significant because it was the first time an actual hole was used as a target.

Further evidence suggests that *kolf* was an early form of golf; Van Hengel illustrated his book with paintings and drawings by renowned Dutch artists like Jan Steen, De Hooch and Van de Neere which clearly show the similarities in style of play and the type of clubs used. Van Hengel also surmised that *kolf* was introduced into Scotland in the fourteenth century by Dutch merchants during trading voyages between Holland and the east coast ports of Edinburgh and Leith. With weather in the North Sea unpredictable and hazardous, especially in winter, journeys could last for weeks, even months. It would have been common practice for Dutch sailors to bring over clubs and balls to avail themselves of their favorite pastime. Evidence also exists showing *kolf* was later played at Cleve in Germany in 1660, and Rome in 1662.

There are also well-documented records of large numbers of feather golf balls being exported from Holland to Scotland in the mid-sixteenth century. Of course Scottish traditionalists will counter with the evidence of the volume of long-nose clubs travelling in the opposite direction. While undoubtedly a substantial amount of trade existed between Edinburgh and the Hague in the fifteenth century, it is open to question whether Dutch merchants brought golf to Scotland or the other way round. A painting by Flemish artist Adriane Van de Velde, dated 1668, clearly shows a group of 'kolfers' standing ready to play on a frozen lake near Haarlem, and just as clearly, they are wearing Scottish kilts.

Apart from the *Book of Hours*, little evidence exists that shows kolf was being played to a finish inside a hole. Indeed, as the illustration dates from around 1500, it is possible that Simon Bennink was depicting a game he could have easily seen at Leith in Scotland. As for the paintings of frozen river scenes in Holland, they only ever show wooden posts driven into the ice to act as targets. The suggestion that these ornately carved posts were stolen at some point, leaving only a hole,

is just a myth. Target posts were still being used in Holland three centuries after holes were first used in Scotland.

Compared with the doubtful claims of ancient pastimes to be the origin of golf, Van Hengel's belief that the two sports were linked is impossible to dismiss. With remarkable skill and diligence he cut a swathe through a mountain of Dutch archive material to give factual backing to his ideas. Unfortunately, anyone now attempting to prove that Scotland is the birthplace of golf has by comparison almost nothing to go on. With the Scottish archives proving to be far less illuminating than the ancient Dutch records, the origins of golf

Below: *A page from a Flemish Book Of Hours dating from the early sixteenth century. It shows the game being played on open ground rather than on ice.*

In 1886, golf author Sir Walter Simpson offered the romantic notion that golf was invented by a bored Scottish shepherd who, while tending his flock, aimed a well-struck blow at a pebble with his crook and watched in amazement as it disappeared down a rabbit hole. Mentally weighing up the chances of repeating such a feat, the shepherd set up for his next shot and did it again. The next day the common links land was awash with shepherds attempting to do the same, and from that moment on the game of golf was born.

A fanciful enough tale but perhaps not as far from the truth as it sounds. Since early times, common links land has been used for golf. Many of the world's most famous golf courses, including St Andrews, are situated between town and sea. At St Andrews the land itself was originally submerged by the sea, before centuries of sand and silt brought in by the tide gradually built up and pushed back the area covered by water. This newly reclaimed area of shoreline took its name from its geographical location – the area linking the land to the sea – and became known as links-land.

Apart from being uniquely suited to the game of golf, the land was of little use for anything else. The sandy soil made it bad farming land, while the wiry grass which barely covered the surface never grew long enough for good grazing for cattle and sheep. Long before someone had the idea of playing golf on it, the 'links' had been designated as common land. Townspeople used it to hold fairs, play sports, even hang their washing – or perhaps more significantly, use it for archery practice.

As mentioned in Chapter One, King James II banned golf and football in 1457 because it interfered with his subjects' compulsory archery practice. Curiously, an earlier statute in 1424 forbade the playing of football for exactly the same reason, but without any mention of golf. This offers the possibility that golf was first played at some point between those two dates, a suggestion which many golf historians dismiss, maintaining that with communication being almost non-existent in fifteenth-century Scotland, the chances of golf becoming so widespread and popular in just over 33 years were very remote indeed. Certainly, from the fourteenth century onwards Scotland was a battle-scarred nation ruled by a succession of child-kings and power-

*King Iames the Second* in the zeir. And that the fute-bal and golfe be vtterly cryed downe, and not to be vfed. And that the bow-markes be maid at ilk Parifh Kirk a pair of Buttes, & fchutting be vfed. And that ilk man fchutte fex fchottes at the leaft, vnder the paine to be rayfed vpon them, that cummis not the leaft, twa pennyes to be giuen to them, that cummis to the bow-markes to drinke. And this to be vfed fra *Pafche* till *Alhallow-mes* afte And be the nixt Midfommer to be reddy with all their graith withou failzie. And that there be a bower and a fledgear in ilk head town of the Schire, And that the toun furnifh him of ftuffe and graith, after as nece him thereto, that they may ferue the countrie with. And as tuitching the futeball and the golfe, to be punifhed be the Barronnis vn-law, and g he takis not the vn-law, that it be taken be the Kingis officiaris. And g

hungry nobles. But the fact remains that the game of golf was popular enough by the mid-fifteenth century to warrant a Scottish Royal Act of Parliament to suppress it.

As well as banning golf and football, the 1457 Act ordered that archery practice be now compulsory in every town churchyard. Hoping to bring the errant townspeople off the links-land where they continued to play both sports, archery ranges were quickly established in kirk-yards across the east coast of Scotland. There, under the watchful eye of the Church of Scotland, each man was ordered to 'schutte six schottes at the least'. Failure to obey the law resulted in a fine of two pennies (the money raised was to be spent on drinks for those who did comply). However, if the King's intention was to force golf off the links, it did not work. Golfers just played in the churchyards instead.

By the late fifteenth century, the local kirk was an integral part of Scottish life. Apart from offering spiritual comfort, the church acted as an important focus for most social activities. With communities scattered across the countryside and linked by dirt track roads, the local church could be as much as a half-day's journey for some people. The Sabbath became a time to meet with friends and neighbors after the service and enjoy each other's company. For the men this would involve playing sports like catch-ball, kypey (marbles) and bowls – and almost certainly golf.

Left: *Originally set down on parchment, the Act by James II stating, 'that fute-bal and golfe be utterly cryed downe' was published in book form in 1560. The earliest known reference to golf, the royal act banned the game in Scotland as it was interfering with his subjects' compulsory archery practice. While the original Act was never officially repealed, the ban on golf became effectively meaningless after 1500 when King James IV took up the game himself.*

Above: *The 8th hole at Royal Aberdeen.*

Perhaps at this point it is important to have some idea of how the game was played. It is generally accepted that the earliest form of golf was a shorter, more restricted version of the game which is played today. Evidence suggests that this was a one-club game, played to a series of targets or 'holes' ranging from fifty to one hundred yards.

In 1471, the ban on golf was repeated, as it was 20 years later in 1491, when it was ordained, 'that in na place of the realm be usit fut bawwis, gouff or uthir sic unproffitable

sports...'. Describing golf as an unprofitable sport illustrates the frustrating time the Scottish authorities were having controlling golf's widespread popularity. Played in almost every major town from Edinburgh in the south to Aberdeen in the north, golf was proving impossible to put down. Finally, after four decades of Scottish royalty trying to suppress the game, King James IV took up golf himself and so the ban became meaningless.

By the early 1500s golf was the game of King and commoner. Peace with England also offered a welcome period of stability for Scotland and over the next century golf's popularity grew at a rapid rate. Primitive golf courses were established at Leith and Bruntsfield in Edinburgh, as well as in other locations all over the east coast of Scotland including St Andrews, Perth, Montrose, Leven, Dornoch, Banff, Aberdeen and even the Orkney Islands in the far north. Apart from a gradual return to the links, the 'shorter' game continued to be played in the town churchyards. At first the attitude of the church authorities was reasonably fair minded. Whilst not approving of golf being played on the Sabbath, it rebuked only those who played 'in tyme of sermonis...'. However, from 1580 onwards, religious

Below: *A bird's eye view of the Old Course at St Andrews.*

intolerance hardened, and the Scottish Church began to look upon golf as unsympathetically as King James II had done over a century before. In a growing age of religious bigotry, pastimes such as golf were denounced from the pulpit as being sinful, and the playing of golf was legislated against. In February 1610, the South Leith Kirk Session stated that:

'There shall be no public playing permitted on the Sabbath days such as playing at bowls, at the penny stone, archery, golf... And if any be found playing publicly in a yard or in fields upon the Sabbath day from morning until evening they shall pay 20 shillings to the poor and also make their public repentance from the pulpit.'

A few years earlier St Andrews Kirk Sessions had fined a number of offenders for playing golf 'in tyme of fast and preching'. A fixed tariff of charges was established, including 10 shillings for a first offence, rising to 20 shillings for the second and 'fault publick repentance' for the third.

Despite the Church's attitude it was known that some clergymen were golfers themselves. The *Historie of the Kirk in Scotland*, published in 1842, revealed the dramatic story of the Bishop of Galloway who, whilst playing golf on Leith Links in 1619, inexplicably had a vision of two men attacking him. Having accepted the position of Bishop after initially denying

that he would, the venerable gentleman took this as an indication of his own wrongdoing. Racked with guilt, he reportedly threw down his clubs, took to his bed and died there. In contrast, the Minister of St Andrews, Robert Blair, had few such misgivings about golf; famous for decorating his sermons with golfing terms, he often compared the union between God and the Church as strong as the joint between club-head and shaft.

Golf continued to be played in Scottish churchyards well into the mid-seventeenth century, but judicial records show it was becoming more dangerous. In 1632, the tragic death of Thomas Chatto of Kelso was reported after he had been hit in the chest by a golf ball. Chatto, who was described as 'lurking in the churchyard while golf was in progress' was hit 'under his left lung' by 'ane deidlie straik'.

With the increasing usage of the feather ball, golf would soon expand beyond the restricted confines of the Scottish churchyard onto the links. It had been a difficult birth but by the beginning of the seventeenth century the game of golf was established and thriving. The earliest years still remain shrouded in mystery. Church and State records offer no idea of how the game began, or even how it was played – they only show how the relevant authorities reacted to its obviously widespread appeal. Whatever the truth, golf in Scotland survived the combined efforts of successive Kings, local Parliament and the Kirk Sessions to become one of the world's great sports.

Right: *Two feathery golf balls from the mid-nineteenth century. They were often stamped with the makers' names – Old Tom Morris's is on the left.*

Above: *Charles I receiving news of the 1641 Irish rebellion whilst playing golf on Leith links.*

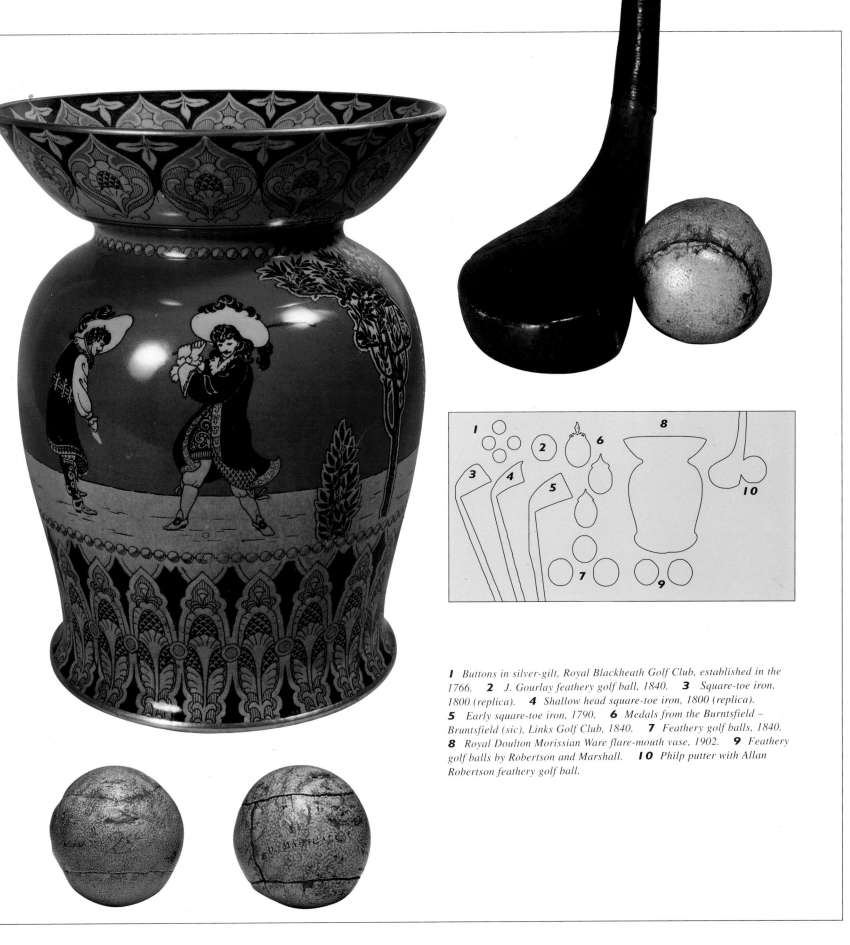

**1** Buttons in silver-gilt, Royal Blackheath Golf Club, established in the 1766. **2** J. Gourlay feathery golf ball, 1840. **3** Square-toe iron, 1800 (replica). **4** Shallow head square-toe iron, 1800 (replica). **5** Early square-toe iron, 1790. **6** Medals from the Burntsfield – Bruntsfield (sic), Links Golf Club, 1840. **7** Feathery golf balls, 1840. **8** Royal Doulton Morissian Ware flare-mouth vase, 1902. **9** Feathery golf balls by Robertson and Marshall. **10** Philp putter with Allan Robertson feathery golf ball.

Above: *James IV of Scotland, who confirmed the 1457 Act banning golf before taking up the game himself.*

Right: *James III of Scotland (1451–1488).*

**G**olf is widely referred to as the Royal and Ancient Game – Ancient because of the five hundred years it has been played in one form or another, and Royal because of its equally long association with the Kings and Queens of Scotland. But while successive Scottish monarchs ratified Acts which forbade their subjects to play golf, they had few inhibitions about playing the game themselves.

The first King of Scotland to play golf was James IV. Like his predecessors, James I and James II, he had little affection for golf in the early years of his reign. Denouncing the game as an 'unprofitable sport' he had confirmed the original ban on golf with one of his own in 1491. Despite this, he was consistently petitioned by nobles from his own court, sympathetic to the golfing cause, to lift the ban on the game. Whatever his political reasons may have been, the King maintained his personal opposition by describing golf as a 'ridiculous sport, requiring neither strength or skill, and properly should be abandoned'.

After decades of conflict, James IV signed the Treaty of Glasgow with Henry VII of England in 1502. The peace that followed brought a rare period of calm to Scotland and the question of playing golf arose once more. The story passed down through the centuries tells how the King was finally persuaded to hit a few golf balls for himself on the lawn at Holyroodhouse. With various lords and barons looking on anxiously, a feathery ball was teed-up on a pinch of sand, but after the first few royal swings it had failed to move. In the nervous silence that must have followed, James IV walked off and resolved to try again the next morning in private. Frustrated at his inability to play such a 'ridiculous sport', the King persevered with his practice, only this time with far greater success. Soon he was hooked – the golfing bug had bitten him and James IV became an enthusiastic convert.

Whether this story is more myth than fact, royal accounts for 1502 show that James IV purchased his first 'golf clubbes' from a bowmaker in Perth. One year later, in 1503, he was known to have spent the whole of February in Edinburgh playing golf and hunting. The lord high treasurer's accounts show several more purchases of clubs, as well as three French crowns, 'to play golf with the Earl of Bothwell'. They were almost certainly payment for a lost wager on the match, for James IV had most of his golfing debts paid from the public purse.

Despite becoming a keen player himself, James IV still refused to lift the ban on golf imposed over half a century earlier. Perhaps aware of the fragile peace with England, archery practice remained compulsory, but the ban on golf had long ceased to have any meaning, and with King James himself a regular visitor to the links, golf prospered in Scotland for over a decade. Peace between the two traditional enemies, England and Scotland, meant that for the first time in half a century, golf could be played openly and without fear of prosecution. Sadly for James IV the truce with England proved short-lived, and his life was tragically cut short at Flodden in 1513.

To his credit, there is evidence that before his death James IV helped introduce golf into England. Married to Princess Elizabeth, daughter of King Henry VII, he was a constant visitor at the English Court. In August 1513, Catherine of Aragon wrote to Cardinal Wolsey at Hampton Court informing him that while 'I shall not so often hear from the King … I thank God I am busy with the golfe'.

James V of Scotland (1512–1542) was taught golf from an early age at the insistence of his father, James IV. In later years he found time to establish his own private links at Gosford in East Lothian. Known to have played many times with his great friend, the Earl of Wemyss, James had a dual purpose for choosing Gosford. Apart from being ideal golfing country, it allowed him to visit three mistresses, all within a short horseride away. History also records that James V ordered that only wooden-headed clubs were to be used – iron-headed clubs, he felt, would tear up the grass!

Mary, Queen of Scots (1542–1587), was also reared in the golfing tradition. Having learned to play from an early age, she

Right: *James VI of Scotland and I of England.*
*He is credited with establishing the first golf course outside Scotland,*
*at Blackheath near London.*

continued with the sport while away at school in France. Students at her Paris school were ordered to carry her clubs. Cadet (pronounced 'cad-day,) is probably where the word 'caddie' comes from.

It was also during Mary's lifetime – in 1552 – that the golf course at St Andrews was first recorded. (Mary was thought to have played there on many occasions.) Unfortunately for Mary, her love of golf aided her downfall and gave Elizabeth I reason enough to send her to the block. After a long period of imprisonment, Mary was finally brought to trial. Known as a devout Catholic, the main role of the prosecutors was to discredit her in the eyes of the English people. The main evidence at her trial was given by Mary's half-brother, the Earl of Moray. In December 1568, he testified that a few days after her husband's death she played 'golf and pall-mall in the fields beside Seton after which 'she did abuse her body with Bothwell', Mary's lover and the suspected murderer of Darnley, her husband.

Whichever accusation did the greatest harm we shall never know. It was enough to condemn her in the eyes of the English court and Mary was put to death soon after. Fortunately, the royal line of succession was still held by keen golfers. Queen Mary's son, James VI of Scotland (1567–1625), was made King after his mother's death in 1587. An enthusiastic golfer, he had learnt to play golf at North Inch in Perth before succeeding Elizabeth I to the English throne (she had left no heirs of her own and he was her closest relation). Crowned James I of England in 1603, he is credited with having established the first golf course outside Scotland.

Early in his reign, he and some friends left his court at Greenwich and went stag hunting at nearby Blackheath, eight miles south of London. Perhaps intrigued by the sandy soil of the heath, or frustrated at being unable to play his favorite pastime, the King reputedly marked out a rough seven-hole course. Little is known about how the King and his companions played except that James and his colleagues struggled around this improvised links using 'hockey-shaped sticks and feather balls'.

Above: *Mary, Queen of Scots, learned to play golf at an early age and continued to play the sport when she was sent away to the French court. Generally acknowledged as the first woman golfer, she was thought to have been a regular visitor to St Andrews.*

Above: *An early long-nosed wood made by Simon Cossar of Leith.*

As well as his passion for paying the game, James I took an interest in the developing trade in golfing equipment. Ten years after establishing the first English course at Blackheath, the King placed an embargo on the amount of feather balls imported from the Continent. Aware of the substantial amount of money disappearing abroad each year, he stated that 'no small quantity of gold and silver is transported yearly out of his Heines' kingdom of Scotland for buying golf balls'. Unfortunately no indication is given as to the source of the trade in feather balls, but most likely it was Holland.

Looking to protect the interests of his fellow countrymen, in 1618 he granted an exclusive 21-year monopoly for the making of golf balls to Quartermaster James Melville. This followed the appointment over ten years earlier of William Mayne, 'bower-burgess' of Edinburgh, as royal club-maker for life.

Not surprisingly, both of King James I's sons, Henry and Charles, took up the game at a young age. Tragically, his eldest son, Henry, died of typhoid at the age of eighteen but not before he made his mark on golf history. The Prince was practising his swing under the watchful eye of a schoolmaster. The young Prince warned the teacher to stand back in case he struck him on his back-swing. Obviously a little deaf, the master failed to move. By now the Prince had swung his club back and a schoolmate called out, 'Beware you do not hit Master Newton!' Henry angrily turned to his friend, saying, 'Had I done so, I had put paid my debts', surely a feeling most golfers have experienced at one time or other!

On Henry's death, his younger brother Charles (1600 – 1649) was crowned King. A tragic historical figure, he was known to have been playing golf on Leith links when news of the Irish Rebellion was brought to him in 1642. He is also reported to have played at Newcastle-upon-Tyne while being held captive by the Scots four years later. History does not record if he finished either round.

After Charles I lost his throne and head after the bloody civil war against Cromwell's Parliamentary forces, his younger son James was exiled to France. Later, in 1682, he returned to England on the death of his brother, King Charles II, and was crowned King a short time later. Apart from playing his part in the Restoration of Charles II, James II (1633–1701) is famous for taking part in golf's first international match. As the young Duke of York during his father's reign, he became involved in a heated debate with two English noblemen about the origins of golf. They insisted that golf was an English game while James stoutly argued for Scotland as the birthplace of golf. Finally the dispute became so acrimonious that it was decided the matter should be settled on the golf course. The challenge was set; the two English nobles would play James and any Scotsman of his choice around Leith links for the honor of their respective nations.

After careful research, the Duke chose for his partner a cobbler called John Paterson. An accomplished player and local champion, Paterson performed well enough to help thrash the English pair. Honor satisfied, a delighted Duke of York presented him with enough money to buy a house in the Canongate area of Edinburgh. Ever mindful of his new fame as the golfing partner to royalty, James Paterson had a coat-of-arms fixed to one of the walls bearing the motto, 'Far and Sure'. It is the same motto the Royal and Ancient Golf Club of St Andrews uses today.

Golf continued throughout the eighteenth century as a game for all classes. After the demise of the Stuart line in 1714, royal golfers became less in evidence. The Young Pretender, Bonnie Prince Charlie, made an abortive attempt to seize the English throne in 1745, but sadly finished his days in exile playing golf in the Borghese Gardens in Rome. Other royals would play golf in the next two centuries, but none would ever have the huge influence over the game as their ancestors had done.

# FEATHERY TO GUTTIE

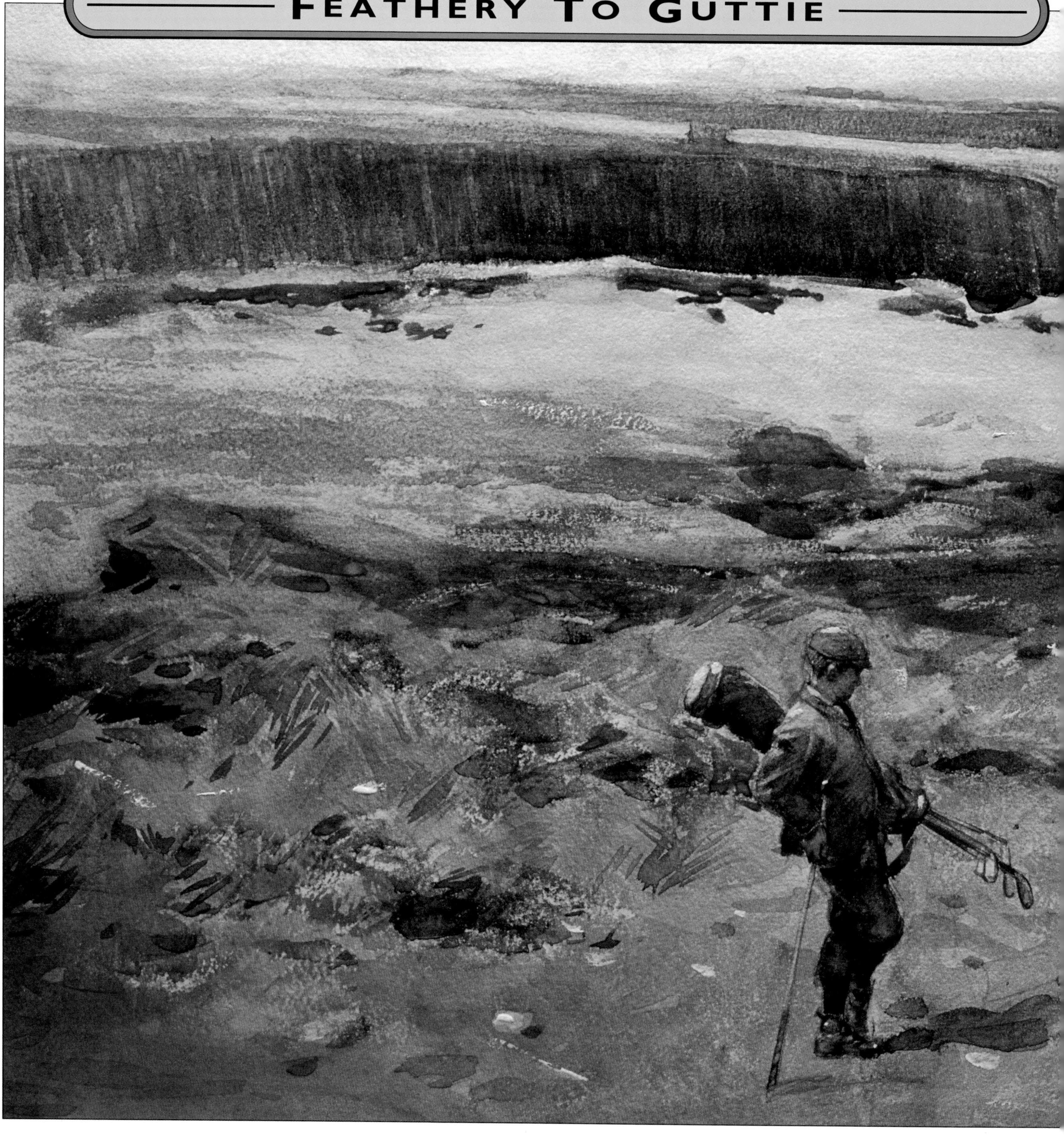

*This 1890's painting depicts a golfer about to attempt the fearsome Cardinal Bunker at Prestwick. The bunker's face is high, steep and faced with timber.*

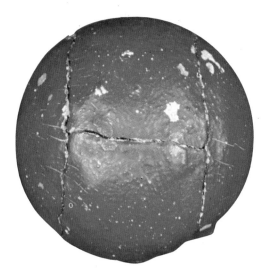

Above: *A feathery from 1830. It was painted red for use in snowy or frosty conditions.*

Above: *A leather-covered feathery stuffed with goose feathers, dating from the mid-nineteenth century.*

The single most important influence on the early history of golf was the feather golf ball. Until the advent of the guttie ball from 1848, the 'feathery' had reigned supreme for almost four centuries. Taking its name from the chicken or goose feathers used as filling, it was thought to have descended from the *paganica* ball of early Roman times. Compared to the first primitive balls made from wood and lead, the feather ball was a miracle of control. Having revolutionized the way golf was played in its formative years, it is doubtful whether the game itself would have survived without it.

Dutch records show that feather balls were first introduced into Scotland from Holland in the late 1480s. Whether they had been introduced even earlier is not certain, but golf had obviously achieved some popularity by then, if records for the amount of imported feather balls is anything to go by. Toll-registers for Bergen op Zoom show that in 1486 a merchant called Richard Clays paid six groats for exporting a barrel-load of golf balls to Scotland! With feather ball-making already an age-old profession in Holland, further records show that large numbers of golf balls continued to be imported into Scotland up until the early seventeenth century.

In 1618 King James VI of Scotland invoked prohibitive tarriffs at all Scottish ports. Later the same year, he granted James Melville an exclusive 21-year monopoly on the making and selling of feather balls throughout the country. What Melville did to deserve this singular honor is unknown. As Quartermaster to the Earl of Morton, it is unlikely that he made the balls himself but rather leased out the rights to others.

His patent established, James Melville placed work all over Scotland on the condition that every ball produced must have his name stamped on it. This was in full accordance with the terms of his contract with the King, and if any 'illegal' ball was found to have been made he was fully entitled to 'seek out and confiscate it'. In a fairly wide-ranging agreement, the only restriction placed on him was the selling price of each ball, where it was decreed that no feather ball should not exceed 'four shillings money of this realme'.

James Melville's freedom to 'lease out his right to others' was an important aspect of his monopoly. Demand was strong and the feather ball was notoriously difficult and time-consuming to make. The actual physical work involved was arduous and demanding, while the constant exposure to lead paints and feather dust actively encouraged chronic chest problems and premature death; even three hundred years later, Victorian ballmakers were only able to produce four to six balls in a day and were prone to the same illnesses as their predecessors.

The ball itself consisted of three sections of untreated bull's hide soaked in alum. It was then stitched together with waxed twine, leaving a small gap through which the boiled feathers could be inserted at a later stage. The leather pouch was then turned inside out, with the smoother surface facing outwards and then the pulped goose or chicken feathers were stuffed inside. The process was easy at first, then as the ball became filled it became increasingly harder. With the ball almost near completion, a long iron brogue fitted with a wooden cross handle was pressed hard against the ballmaker's chest so that extra pressure could be applied. Once the ball was roughly round, a final stitch closed the seam and sealed in the mixture. If the ball appeared misshapen at any point, it was rounded with one or two blows from a heavy hammer.

Once left out to dry, simple physics took over – the bull's hide contracted while the boiled feathers inside expanded. After two days more, the result was a hard, solid ball. The ball was then painted with a white lead-based paint used to protect the ball against moisture. Once dry, it was stamped with the ballmaker's name and offered for sale.

After Melville's monopoly expired many of the originally contracted ballmakers set up in business for themselves. In 1642, John Dickson was appointed by Aberdeen Town Council to make and sell feather balls in the district. Interestingly enough, it had been two other Dicksons from Leith – William and Thomas – who had years before accused James Melville of 'pretending he has a gift from his Majesty's late father, for exacting a certain impost aff everie gowffe ball made within this kingdome'.

Taken before the Edinburgh Privy Council in 1629, they accused Melville of using strong-arm tactics in attempting to enforce his monopoly. They claimed he had ordered 'lawlesse souldiers' to confiscate nineteen feather golf balls from their workshop. Indeed, Melville had been well within his rights to do that under the terms of his contract with King James VI, but the King had died four years earlier, the contract had expired on his death, and the Law Lords found him guilty, fined him and cautioned him.

Unfortunately, no James Melville feather golf balls exist today, but those made by later ballmakers have survived and offer testimony to the amount of skill involved. The most prominent makers of the early nineteenth century were the Gourlays of Leith and Musselburgh. They were acknowledged as master ballmakers during their own lifetime, and it was fashionable during the early 1800s to play only with a 'Gourlay'. They are as equally prized in the modern era by collectors of golfing antiquities, where they often fetch huge sums of money at auction.

Another leading feather ballmaker favored by collectors is Allan Robertson of St Andrews. Also known as the finest player of his generation, he led the way in quality and output for many years – producing 2,456 balls in 1844 alone. Robertson was also the mentor of 'Old' Tom Morris, employing him as his

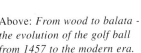
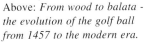
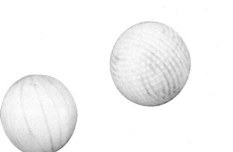

Above: *From wood to balata - the evolution of the golf ball from 1457 to the modern era.*

apprentice for many years. Morris, who later went on to make featheries of his own, became one of the legendary champions of golf.

By the mid-1840s, the feather ball was seemingly unsurpassable. However, within a few short years it had been made obsolete by a new innovation in golf ball design – the 'guttie'. Made from a latex solution called gutta-percha, it was discovered in 1848 by a St Andrews clergyman, Robert Adam Paterson. He had received an ancient Indian statue of Vishnu through the post packed in gutta-percha for safety. A keen golfer himself, he cut off a small piece, softened it in hot water and molded it by hand into the shape of a ball. The results must have been impressive because he immediately took out a patent and sold the manufacturing rights to a London firm.

Shortly afterwards, author James Balfour wrote to Paterson and requested some gutta balls for a trial. Feather ballmaker John Gourlay watched the trial at Musselburgh and instantly realized his ancient craft was doomed. Having a standing order from his patron, Sir David Baird, to send on as many feather balls as he had in stock, Gourlay immediately posted off six dozen! Probably even before his Lordships supply had been used up, the new guttie ball had established itself in the hearts of Scotland's golfers. As for their pockets, that took even less persuasion!

Below: *Smooth gutta ball dating from 1850.*

Even with a price set under four shillings, the feather ball was prohibitively expensive to buy. In 1840, the average cost of a Gourlay feathery was between four and five shillings which made them unavailable for all but the well-off. The were also known to be unreliable in the rain – a common problem in Scotland – where they quickly became sodden and unplayable. Even for the well-to-do in Scottish society, the cost of replacing one feather ball cut or damaged by a miss-hit shot was a serious matter. The guttie, by comparison, sold at about one-quarter of the feather ball's price and, not surprisingly, it was welcomed with open wallets.

Below: *Top hats and tails: St Andrews in 1855. The group includes Allan Robertson (seventh from the left).*

Despite John Gourlay's reaction there were still considerable problems with the first guttie balls. Smooth and unpainted, they flew badly when new and had a violent tendency to dip in flight. Rumors of their aerodynamic instability were eagerly fuelled by feathery makers like Allan Robertson. Born into his father's ball-making business, he obviously felt he had most to lose from this new ball. In his *Reminiscences of Golf and Golfers*, published in 1890, Thomas Peter recalled asking Robertson to try out the guttie for himself. Robertson, the most skilled golfer of his era, deliberately topped the ball and said it would never fly. Robertson also began paying St Andrews cad-dies sixpence a time to find 'lost' guttie balls and bring them to him for disposal – disposal meaning burning them late at night in his workshop.

However, the final straw came for Allan Robertson when he heard that his old apprentice, Tom Morris, had used gutties on the Old Course. Worse still, they had been given to him by a good customer of his, John Campbell of Saddell. Morris lost his job and the two men hardly spoke to each other again. Soon, the tidal wave of guttie balls was too much even for Allan Robertson to hold back. After the ball was found to fly much better when cut, ballmakers started marking the surface with lines. These 'hand-cut' gutties effectively signaled the final days for the feathery. The economics, as much as anything else, prompted this change – as many gutties could be produced in a day as feather balls in a week.

Allan Robertson eventually came round to the 'new ball.' Shortly before his death in 1859, he realized, too late, that while he could no longer sell golf balls at four shillings each, he could sell far more of the newer, cheaper ones. With his death the golden age of the feather ball maker was effectively over. The first 'mass-produced' ball had arrived and it heralded a new era – an era when millions worldwide would be given the opportunity to play and enjoy the game of golf.

Below: *An early hand-hammered gutta ball from around 1855.*

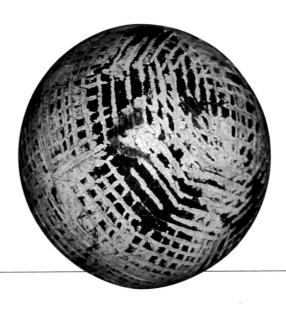

The earliest golf clubs made belong to Royal Troon in Scotland. Originally discovered in a bricked-up closet in Hull, they were found together with a newspaper dated 1741. Whether this is a reliable clue as to how old they are is open to question. Perhaps, more accurately, the six wooden clubs are thought to date from the first quarter of the eighteenth century, while the two irons go back even further. Known worldwide as the 'Ancient Clubs', they are on almost permanent display inside the clubhouse at Troon.

As historic relics of a bygone age they deserve a more detailed portrait. All eight clubs have thick ash shafts. The grips on all but two are missing, but those that have survived are heavily padded and made from coarse wool. The wooden clubs have broad elongated heads with an elaborate crested design on top of the head. All are weighted at the back with lead and have animal bone protecting the leading edge of the face.

Perhaps the two most interesting clubs are the early irons. Fitted with shafts measuring almost three inches in width across the top, they are known descriptively in turn as a 'heavy spur-toe' iron, and a 'square-toe' driving iron. In contrast to the beautifully crafted woods, both irons are cumbersome and heavy, bringing into question just how anyone could have ever used them. With little information available about club-making before 1700, the task of accurately dating these irons becomes a matter of educated guesswork. Blacksmiths were known to have made iron-headed clubs back in the late seventeenth century, but what happened to those clubs used two centuries before?

Below: *Heavy spur-toe irons dating from the late eighteenth century.*

PRESENTED TO THE TROON GOLF CLUB
ADAM WOOD, Esq., of Troon,

The first recorded golf club-maker was William Mayne of Edinburgh. His official appointment in 1603 as royal club-maker for life to King James VI shows the extent of golf's popularity back in the early seventeenth century. William Mayne was described as a 'Bower-burgess', which indicates that his business also included making longbows. This transition from bow-making to golf club craftsmanship, with all its comparative knowledge of woods, has long been accepted as how the first club-makers started. As the longbow declined in favor of gunpowder and shot it would seem to be a natural transition for the longbow-makers to take, but whether this extended to making iron-headed clubs is not so clear.

Around the time of William Mayne, a typical set of clubs varied between three and five long-nose woods, as well as one iron-headed club for difficult 'trouble' shots. Little is known

Above: *With club heads made from thorn, apple, pear and beech, the long-nose wood prevailed throughout the feathery ball era up until the late nineteenth century.*

Left: *The Adam wood collection at Royal Troon Golf Club. The earliest clubs known to exist, they comprise two thick bladed irons and six long-nose woods. They date back to the early 1700s.*

about the purpose of each club but records from the period describe clubs as 'bonker clubbis' (presumably for bunkers) 'scrapers' and 'tin-face' irons. Most golfers carried at least one 'trouble' club but, because of the fragile nature and high cost of the feather ball, it was hardly ever used. Too easily cut or damaged by the thick-bladed irons, it was only in the direst of situations that they would even be considered. In later years sturdy, round-headed 'rut' irons were introduced. Also known as 'track' irons, they were designed to help extract the golf ball from the horse-drawn carriage tracks which often lined the fairway.

From the era of William Mayne until the advent of the harder guttie ball in 1848, the majority of the golfers' clubs were invariable made up of long-nose woods. Unfortunately, no clubs made by Mayne or any of his contemporaries like James Pett of St Andrews have survived to this day, but the style in which

they were fashioned is thought to have lasted well into the nineteenth century.

These early wooden-headed clubs had a slender, pear-shaped appearance and were known collectively as 'long-nose' woods. Unlike the crude iron clubs, they proved perfectly suitable for sweeping the feather ball. Described as having a 'greyhound neck with a snake-like head', the earliest known heads were made from thorn wood with beech, apple and pear following many years later. The striking face had a slightly concave or hooked appearance, while the back of the head was fitted with lead for extra weight. For protection against the sharp flint pebbles found on links-land, a thin strip of ramshorn or bone was inserted into the lower edge of the striking face.

The head was attached to the shaft by means of a long-angled joint called a 'scar' or 'splice.' The earliest shafts were made from seasoned ash, but greenheart, lancewood, purpleheart and bloomahoo were all used according to taste. Hickory was introduced many years later in the early nineteenth century and proved to be the most resilient wood of all. The shaft was shaped by hand and bonded together with the club-head using a powerful animal glue, then finally it was sealed with waxed twine or whipping. The average length of the shaft was longer than it is today, varying from 40 to 45 inches (1.02–1.14 metres).

The grip was usually made from sheepskin or leather, padded out with a coarse wool underlayer. The final color of club-head depended solely on the type of wood that was used. In the era immediately after William Mayne's, unpolished thorn heads were rubbed with a red dye or 'keel' to protect them against the harsh Scottish weather. In later years, the head was lovingly polished then treated with a hare's foot dipped in a mixture of varnish and oil.

Below: *To protect the underside of the club from damage, rams'-horn was inserted into the leading edge and fixed with wooden pegs.*

Above: *Robert Forgan (seated) in his St Andrews workshop. It was he who bridged the gap between the old long-nose wood makers and the new age of mass-production.*

At some point in the late eighteenth century, the actual maker's name or mark was stamped on top of the head for identification. This alone was symptomatic of golf's rising popularity in the mid-eighteenth century. As golf grew in popularity, club-makers become fashionable in their own right, with golfers looking to purchase only those clubs with the 'right' name.

The first maker to mark his clubs was James McEwan in 1770. Stamping his clubs 'J. McEwan' with a thistle above the name, he was the most respected club-maker of his period. He was followed by Simon Cossar of Leith in around 1785 and John Jackson of Perth in 1820.

The club-maker's art began to thrive during the latter part of the eighteenth century. Simon Cossar was already official club-maker to the fledgling Honourable Company of Edinburgh Golfers at Leith, while others like Henry Miln at St Andrews and Thomas Comb and Andrew Bailey at Brunsfield all prospered with the advent of the first organized golf societies. In the half century which followed, the artisans responsible for producing these early woods can be categorized into two distinct groups – the golf professionals and the craftsmen.

The golf professional's club-making business was built almost solely on his reputation as a player. He had other responsibilities, like teaching and greenkeeping, and for the most part the clubs that carried his name were usually the product of a skilled apprentice. In the mid-eighteenth century, legendary golfers like Tom Morris Senior, Willie Park and the Dunn brothers all fell into this category.

By comparison the craftsman had little involvement with competitive golf. Often trained as carpenters, wheelwrights or cabinetmakers, most had a thorough knowledge of wood and used that knowledge to produce some of the finest clubs ever made. Hugh Philp, for example, was a St Andrews joiner by trade who repaired golf clubs in his spare time. By 1819 his reputation was such that the Society of St Andrews Golfers (later to become The Royal and Ancient) appointed him as their official club-maker. Described as a 'dry-haired man, rather gruff to strangers', Hugh Philp was the master craftsman of his time. Celebrated during his own lifetime, woods marked with 'H. Philp' were often copied by unscrupulous forgers eager to make a sale.

In the final years of the feather ball era, Hugh Philp's skill in putter-making was unsurpassed. From his small workshop near the Old Course in St Andrews, each individual putter club-head would be lovingly smoothed, polished and waxed, not once or twice but thirty or forty times. Golfers from all over Scotland, including other professionals like Tom Morris, Willie Park and George Daniel Brown, would flock to his workshop in St Andrews to purchase a club from the master craftsman.

Hugh Philp employed many apprentices, like James Wilson, who went on to become famous club-makers in their own right. After the introduction of the guttie ball in 1848, Philp despaired of making long-nose woods resilient enough to resist the harder ball. Increasingly, many golfers returned their cracked and ruined 'Philp' woods, only to be rebuked by the master for risking them in so foolhardy a way.

Around 1852, Hugh Philp took on his nephew, Robert Forgan, with the obvious intention of handing on his business to him. Forgan in turn proved the best choice possible. After Philp died in 1856, he expanded the small business into one of the largest golf club manufacturing concerns in the world. The passing of Hugh Philp effectively signalled the end of an era. The feather ball, which had been in constant use for almost four centuries, had been made obsolete by the new guttie. And although it would take a little longer, the era of the long-nose wood was also drawing to an end. Since the early days of William Mayne and Simon Cossar, club-making had been associated with craftsmanship and individuality. From 1860 onwards, club-making would change to mass-production and uniformity. The days of the skilled club-maker were, sadly, over.

*Below: Hugh Philp was appointed official club-maker to the Society of St Andrews Golfers (later the Royal & Ancient) in 1819.*

Up until the mid-eighteenth century, golf was still a relatively classless game. The street urchin with his bent stick and supply of pebbles was as common a sight on the links as the wealthy merchant with his long-nose woods and stock of feather balls. But golf was no longer the primitive game that it once was, and social attitudes were changing along with the times.

By 1740, strong trading links with Holland and France had brought a period of relative prosperity to Scotland. Many Edinburgh merchants had made their fortune from wool and cotton and enjoyed the privileges and respect their wealth had brought. With golf a favored pastime, it was natural to want this

Below: *'Jaimie', a North Berwick caddy painted by John Robertson Reid. Prior to the introduction of the golf bag in the 1890s, caddies would carry the golf clubs under their arms in a bundle.*

privilege and respect extended to the links. Banding together with others of the same class and social standing they began to segregate themselves into small groups. Having the time and money to spend on their leisure activities, these 'Gentleman golfers' were able to indulge in the habit of arranging matches during weekdays – something that the humble artisans could never afford to do.

Another factor which led to the widening gap between the ordinary people and these gentleman golfers was the use of caddies. A typical set of clubs at this time numbered approximately five long-nose woods and one iron. Before the introduction of a golf bag in the late nineteenth century, the clubs were carried underarm in a bundle and placed on the ground between shots. Local townspeople were employed to perform this task and for many it became a useful way to supplement a fairly meager existence. Naturally, the poorer classes could never afford caddies themselves, or even the expensive clubs and feather balls they carried around. The well-to-do golfers who could were now easily distinguishable and given due deference by other users on the links. While the high and low of Scottish society continued to play golf at Bruntsfield and Leith, there were now accepted distinctions. The gentleman golfers remained a select band, while tradesman and artisans considered themselves superior to the growing sub-class of caddies, ballmakers and club-makers.

'Match Days' became a regular occurrence on the golf links around Edinburgh. Leith rapidly became the focus for Scottish society, with businessmen, lairds, clergymen, lawyers, military officers and the landed gentry all gathering there to play golf. Essentially a time for social intercourse, these friends would complete their day by retiring to the private room of a local tavern for a hearty meal. With a strong masonic influence underlying the whole occasion, these postmatch feasts became a regular feature of match days at Leith and nearby Bruntsfield. It became the time for ritualized speech making, holding inquests into the day's play, making and settling wagers and, above all, drinking copious amounts of fine wine and port. Describing the early excesses of the gentleman golfers of Leith, Tobias Smollett –

a contemporary golf chronicler – recorded that 'they never went to bed without each having the best of part of a gallon of claret inside his belly'.

It was only a matter of time before these groups of like-minded friends became organized into the first official clubs and societies. One of the earliest, the Royal Burgess Society, is thought to have began in 1735. The first members played golf over the short five-hole course at Bruntsfield links. Now little more than a sad patch of land under the shadow of Edinburgh Castle, in the mid-eighteenth century it was a thriving open space enjoyed by all the inhabitants of the city.

The Royal Burgess Society took its membership from a wide cross-section of Edinburgh's citizens. Unlike the 'gentleman golfers' that made up the ranks of the Honourable Company and Society of St Andrews Golfers, almost half at the Royal Burgess were lawyers, with the remainder comprising bankers, architects, stone-masons, bakers, grocers, hairdressers, glaziers and ropemakers. Club business was conducted from the 'Golf House' tavern owned by club-maker Thomas Comb. Rooms were leased for their private dinners, while locker rooms were made available to the members. Long before the days of custom-built clubhouses, this proved a welcome sanctuary where

Above left: *William St Clair of Roslin. A leading figure in the formation of the Honourable Company of Edinburgh Golfers, he was elected captain in 1761, 1766, 1770 and 1771.*

Left: *Blackheath golfer and caddy from 1790. Note the bottle of brandy tucked into the caddy's coat pocket - it was there in case a tipple was needed between holes!*

Right: *William Inglis, captain of the Honourable Company of Edinburgh golfers from 1782 to 1784.*

37

the members could change from their daily clothes into their official golfing uniform.

An important element in the growing segregation of the early club golfers were the uniforms which were worn by almost every formal golf society in Scotland. Originally they were little more than adapted fox-hunting jackets, so not surprisingly the most common choice of a club color was red. Around 1780, the Society of St Andrews Golfers agreed on a red club jacket with gold buttons, buff-colored golfing 'frock' and scarlet cap. In contrast the Edinburgh Burgess had red jackets with a black collar similar to the Blackheath Club in London. There were odd exceptions like grey uniforms for Glasgow golfers, but generally most clubs stayed with scarlet red. Perhaps recognizing the importance of ceremony in attracting respect from other golfers on the links, club members were often fined nominal amounts if they were not properly attired. In 1837 John Wood of the Honourable Company was penalized two tappit hens for appearing on Leith links without his golfing jacket!

The Royal Burgess was joined in 1761 with the newly formed Bruntsfield Links Golfing Society, made up from loyal supporters of the exiled Bonnie Prince Charlie. They established their own club because they had little wish to drink the health of King George of England. Little is known about the Scottish rebels that formed the first Bruntsfield Club, but they lived harmoniously with their colleagues at Royal Burgess for over two centuries, first at Bruntsfield itself and then, as the course became overcrowded, at Musselburgh after 1874. Their present-day home is in the Barnton area of Edinburgh.

Next to the Royal and Ancient, the most celebrated private golf club in the world is the Honourable Company of Edinburgh Golfers. They were the probably the most important and influential of the early golf societies. Originally called the Gentleman Golfers of Edinburgh, they played over Leith links from the early 1740s and established the first official club there in 1744. One of the first golf courses known to exist, Leith was a rough five-hole layout built on common land near Edinburgh's important sea-port. In what must have been a

Above: *Golfing attire in the mid-nineteenth century.*

daunting test for golfers using long-nose clubs and feather balls, the original holes measured 414, 461, 426, 495 and 435 yards in distance respectively.

Now based at Muirfield on the Firth of Forth, the Honourable Company's first meeting place was at Lucky Clephan's Inn, close to the links. Later moving to their own Golf House, they were recognized as a more 'ceremonial' club than any other in Scotland. With a strong masonic influence coloring their early years, wining and dining were important ritualistic occasions. Match day dinners were always celebrated with great pomp and formality, where members drank port from silver tankards, and distinguished captains of the society were honored with portraits commissioned and paid for by the other members.

This important connection between the formation of the first golf societies and Freemasonry has remained relatively unexplored, but enough evidence exists to show that many of the early Scottish clubs were actually established by Masons. Records relating to the Royal Burgess show the Club Captain as having the right to elect three members a year 'on the shake of a hand'. Others refer to the masonic initiation that new members went through before being allowed to join. As for the Honourable Company, the foundation stone of the original Golf House was laid by William St Clair of Roslin in the presence of the original committee. The written record of the dedication ceremony offered the masonic rank of all those present; William St Clair was an Hereditary Grand Master of Scotland while all but two others were Master Masons. Similarly at St Andrews, when the foundation stone of the Royal and Ancient clubhouse was laid, it was done with full masonic honors.

However, by the early nineteenth century, many of the earliest 'masonic' clubs including Blackheath and Royal Burgess, were forced by economic circumstances to allow an increasing number of non-masons to become members. During this period, many original club documents were either lost or deliberately destroyed in an attempt to cover over their secretive past. Considered an immeasurable loss, it is only in recent years that the role of the masons has been seen as something positive and beneficial. From what we know of the earliest golf clubs and societies, it is certain many of them would not have survived to this day without masonic contribution.

After 1850, the onset of the Industrial Revolution brought a new realism to Scotland. The ceremony and ritual associated with many private golf clubs was no longer considered appropriate. The advent of the cheaper guttie ball had brought the game within the reach of millions of ordinary people, and golf, not socializing, became the most important consideration. At the end of the eighteenth century there were just ten golf clubs in Scotland and England. By the close of the nineteenth, there would be over two thousand. Golf had come a long way from the early days of the 'Gentleman Golfers of Leith'.

| Earliest Golf Clubs (up to 1800) | | |
|---|---|---|
| I. | The Royal Burgess Golfing Society of Edinburgh | 1735 |
| II. | The Honourable Company of Edinburgh Golfers | 1744 |
| III. | The Royal and Ancient Golf Club of St Andrews | 1754 |
| IV. | Bruntsfield Links Golfing Society | 1761 |
| V. | Royal Blackheath | 1766 |
| VI. | Royal Musselburgh | 1774 |
| VII. | Royal Aberdeen | 1780 |
| VIII. | Crail Golfing Society | 1786 |
| IX. | Glasgow Golf Club | 1787 |
| X. | Dunbar Golf Club | 1794 |
| XI. | Burntisland Golf Club | 1797 |

Below: *A painting by John Wallace from 1895 entitled, 'Saturday morning, Reiss Golf Club, Wick, Caithness'. The golfers featured include the town's mayor, military officer and local solicitor.*

In the mid-eighteenth century, shortly before the formation of the Honourable Company of Edinburgh Golfers, groups of well-to-do friends would meet informally on the links to play for small wagers. These individual matches were contested keenly enough, but the need was felt for a competition in which they could all take part. In March 1744, the gentleman golfers who frequented Leith links petitioned Edinburgh Council to furnish them with a prize. In turn, they would organize a competition. In due course, the Council authorized the city treasurer to make funds available for a silver club to be made, the only condition being that it did not exceed fifteen pounds in value.

This response from Edinburgh Council to the representation of 'several Gentleman of Honour, skilful in the ancient and healthful exercise of the Goff', was indeed a generous one. Conditions were then drawn up for the proposed event, including an entry fee of five shillings from each player, with the accumulated fund going to the eventual winner. The winner would be required to attach a silver ball to the club and would

be designated 'Captain of the Goff' for the forthcoming year, which effectively meant officiating in any dispute that might arise in future competitions.

The records of the fledgling Honourable Company of Edinburgh Golfers note the first winner of the silver club to be Edinburgh surgeon John Rattray. Rattray himself was one of the founder members of the original society and was a fitting winner. More significantly, he helped draw up the thirteen simple rules offered as guidance for all the competitors.

The general conditions for the tournament had already been drawn up by the gentleman golfers and had been approved by Edinburgh Council. They had agreed that competitors should be sent out in pairs or 'by threes if their number be great', but nothing was mentioned about the problems which may have been encountered during play. Golfers familiar with Leith links knew what hazards to expect, but for those taking part from Bruntsfield and St Andrews, some official guidance was needed.

Right: *Attached to the historic golf clubs are the 'Captain's Balls'. Every captain of the Royal and Ancient is expected to donate a silver golf ball in honor of his year in office. Royal captains donate a gold ball.*

Shortly before the event, thirteen rules were written down detailing what action should be taken in any given situation. They were a milestone in the history of golf. One year later they were adopted by the Society of St Andrews Golfers, and today they form the basis by which golf is played all over the world. The Competition for the Silver Club in 1744 was the first ever official tournament held in golf. Played under the Leith Code, the thirteen rules then were:

I.   You must tee your ball within a club's length of the hole.
II.  Your tee must be on the ground.
III. You are not to change the ball before you strike off the tee.
IV.  You are not to remove stones or bones for the sake of playing your ball except upon the fair green, and that only within a club's length of the ball.
V.   If your ball comes among water, or any watery filth, you are at liberty to take out your ball and bringing it behind the hazard and teeing it, you may play it with any club and allow your adversary a stroke for so getting out your ball.
VI.  If your balls be found anywhere touching one another, you are to lift the first ball till you play the last.
VII. At holing, you are to play your ball honestly for the hole, and not to play on your adversary's ball, not lying in your way to the hole.
VIII. If you should lose your ball by its being taken up, or in any other way, you are to go back to the spot where you struck last and drop another ball and allow your adversary a stroke for your misfortune.
IX.  No man at holing his ball is allowed to mark his way to the hole with his club or anything else.
X.   If a ball be stop'd by any person, horse, dog or anything else, the ball so stop'd must be played where it lyes.
XI.  If you draw your club in order to strike, and proceed so far in the stroke as to be bringing down your club – If then your club shall break in anyway, it is accounted to be a stroke.

XII. He whose ball lyes farthest from the hole is obliged to play first.
XIII. Neither trench, ditch or dyke made for the preservation of the links, nor the Scholars' holes, or the Soldiers lines, shall be accounted a hazard, but the ball is to be taken out, teed, and played with any iron club.

Below: *Articles and laws concerning the rules of golf, from 1744.*

Above: *The ancient stone bridge crossing the Swilcanburn at St Andrews.*

It is interesting to see just how many of the rules are still in force today. The rules stipulating how to tee the ball and not marking the line with the club remain unchanged. Penalty strokes are roughly the same: loss of distance and 'allowing your adversary one stroke for the misfortune'. The golfer furthest from the hole still remains the one to play first, and the rule about not deliberately playing your opponent's ball remains the fundamental basis of golf.

There are a few rules that require a little explanation: Rule I for example, deals with teeing the ball up within 'one club's length of the hole'. In 1744 it was normal, that when having putted out, a handful of sand was scooped from the hole and a tee formed for the next shot: this had been common practice since the earliest days of golf. This rule offers some idea of the poor conditions of the greens.

Eventually extended to two club lengths, this rule remained in use until 1875, when separate teeing grounds were introduced.

Another insight into how golf must have been played in the mid-eighteenth century comes from the rule dealing with golf balls being stopped by 'any person, horse, dog, or anything else'. Amazingly, this rule made allowance for all the common 'hazards' of links golf – footballers, grazing animals, horseriders and, most commonly of all, women hanging their washing out to dry! Though membership of the original Honourable Company was limited to those from the same class and social standing, the links themselves were on common land. Distractions like those above were commonplace on every links in Scotland and were accepted as such.

The first competition for the Silver Club went ahead on 2 April 1744, but despite being open to everyone the first tournament attracted little response. Undaunted, the Gentleman Golfers of Edinburgh applied to have the competition restricted to 'such Noblemen and Gentlemen as they approve to be Members of the Company of Golfers'. Edinburgh City Council agreed, and from 1764 the Silver Club could only be won by their own members.

The Honourable Company made Leith its home until the 1820s. By then housing had sprung up around the course and the distractions had become increasingly intolerable. Like the Royal Burgess and Bruntsfield, the Honourable Company left Leith for the coastal resort of Musselburgh, remaining there until 1891, when they made their final move to their present home of Muirfield.

Certainly the world of golf owes John Rattray and his friends a debt of thanks. The importance of those early rules goes far beyond the first competition at Leith. Until that point golf was a chaotic sport played on an ad hoc basis with groups of friends all playing by different rules. It was vital for the development of golf that an established set of rules be published and adhered to by everyone. The late broadcaster and writer Henry Longhurst once said that the rules of golf should be brief enough to be written on the back of a matchbox. Perhaps the 'Leith Code' is still a little wordy for his taste but, compared to the modern interpretation of the rules, the original thirteen are masterpieces of vision and clarity.

Below: *Parading the Silver Club through the streets of St Andrews in 1787.*

19.—CHARLES I.
A Royal and Ancient Golfer.

20.—F. G. TAIT.
Practice of Golf.

21.—H. G. HUTCHINSON.
Literary Golf Champion.

22.—J. H. TAYLOR.
Open Champion 1894-5.

24.—HAROLD HILTON.

25.—J. BALL.
A Celebrated Golf Ball.

26.—TOM MORRIS, JNR.

27.—J. E. LAIDLAY.

28.—PROFESSOR TAIT.
Theory of Golf.

32.—LADY MARGARET
SCOTT.
Lady Champion 1893-4-5.

38.—JOHN TAYLOR.
From a Painting by Raeburn
and W. Gordon.

46.—ALEX. HERD.

2.—TOM MORRIS.
The G.O.M. of Golf.

4.—SANDY SMITH.
North Berwick.

Mr. CRAWFORD.
Caddie and Golf Professor.

14.—"FIERY" OF
MUSSELBURGH.

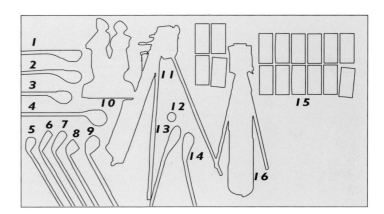

*1 Patrick driving putter, 1860.  2 Philp putter, 1845.  3 Patrick putter, 1895.  4 Bulger driver by E. Morris, 1899.  5 Rut niblick, 1890.  6 Cleek, 1850.  7 Dished-face general iron, 1850. 8 Square-toe iron, 1810.  9 A club designed for playing a ball out of water, 1900  10 'The Golfers' in Stafford china, 1890.  11 Patent golf bag, 1890.  12 Mesh Gutta golf ball, 1890.  13 Replica juvenile play club of 1710.  14 Replica putter of 1750.  15 Copes Golfers, cigarette cards: part of a series of 50, 1910.  16 Patent golf bag, 1890.*

Above: *Golf at St Andrews in 1890, with 'Old' Tom Morris (with beard) standing in the foreground.*

Below: *The golfer and his caddy at the far end of the Old Course, St Andrews, close to the Eden estuary. This illustration comes from a 1890 publication.*

The ancient town of St Andrews may not be the birthplace of golf but it is certainly its spiritual home. Situated on Scotland's windswept east coast, it is a Mecca to golfers from every corner of the globe. Driving along the winding road from the south, one can see the old grey town rises up ahead : the most famous view in golf fills the senses. In the foreground is the legendary 'Road Hole' green with its treacherous slopes and steep-faced bunker. Ahead lies the ancient footbridge which crosses the Swilken burn and the row of shops and private clubrooms that border the eighteenth fairway can be viewed from the road. Finally, at the head of the Old Course itself, stands the majestic stone grey facade of the Royal and Ancient Clubhouse. All the great names of golf have played at the Royal and Ancient: the modern greats, and the legendary champions of the past like Harry Vardon, Walter Hagen and Ben Hogan, Tom Morris Snr, Willie Park, and even Mary, Queen of Scots. St Andrews is the place where golfing history has been made. Nowhere in the world does five centuries of golfing history come to life as it does in St Andrews.

Occupying a narrow finger of land stretching away from the town like a shepherd's crook, the Old Course remains the most famous eighteen holes of golf in the world. The ancient links, situated between St Andrews Bay and the Eden estuary, remain starkly primitive and much as nature had originally shaped it. By modern standards the Old Course at St Andrews is not beautiful. At first sight it appears flat and uninspiring with little of the majestic splendor of Augusta or Pinehurst. The first time Sam Snead saw the course through the window of his railway carriage, he asked a stranger: 'What in the devil is that? It looks like an old abandoned golf course.' To his eternal credit, the stranger replied: 'That, sir, is the Royal and Ancient Golf Club of St Andrews, founded in 1754 and is not now, nor ever will be, abandoned!'

In earlier years another legendary champion who initially found the Old Course not to his liking was Bobby Jones. Having made his Open debut there in 1921, Jones tore up his scorecard in disgust after blowing up with an eight halfway through the third round. Storming off the course he swore never to return. Like Sam Snead, Bobby Jones did return to St Andrews in 1927 to win the second of his three Open Championships. Before his death in 1971, Jones said, 'If I had to play one golf course for the rest of my life it would be the Old Course at St Andrews.'

Despite its almost mythical reputation, the Old Course is not universally liked by everyone. Its gritty, rugged charm which eventually wins over the most vocal of its critics sometimes takes time to work its magic. The ancient links offer pleasure and pain in equal measure – often, all in the space of one hole. Frequently frustrating as it is, many of the world's top golfers have left St Andrews asking what all the fuss is about, while others enthuse about its challenge until their dying day. Of course there are some who miss the point altogether. They are usually the ones who berate the venerable links for having too many blind shots, no buggy paths and not enough 'island greens' !

Below: *Allan Robertson (third from right) watches as Hay Wemyss drives off at St Andrews.*

Above: *Golfers negotiating the Swilcanburn at St Andrews in 1895.*

The majority of the fairways at St Andrews do resemble a green moonscape and rarely, if ever, offer the golfer a flat lie. Apart from the first and eighteenth holes, St Andrews is also plagued with bunkers. As if getting out of them were not difficult enough, they all have evocative names like 'Principal's Nose', 'Lion's Mouth', 'Coffins', and 'Grave'. Never uniform, they vary in size and shape from a large dustbin lid to those like 'Hell' bunker which is big enough to merit its own par.

The problems do not stop at the greens. With double greens on the majority of holes, it becomes a constant source of embarrassment to anyone playing St Andrews for the first time to putt out within the shadow of the other flag. Excuses like, 'I was aiming at the wrong hole' are usually treated with the contempt they deserve. Today, the famous double greens on the Old Course are probably its most visible link with the past. Up until the mid-eighteenth century the narrow strip of land was only wide enough for single fairways and greens. At that time a typical round at St Andrews was 22 holes, with the golfer playing eleven holes straight out, and then the same eleven holes in reverse.

Later, as more people took up the game, it was thought safer to have separate holes for the outward and inward journeys. With no room for eighteen individual greens, a compromise was reached where the same ones were used twice, and just the fairways were widened. Then in 1764, William St Clair played its 22 holes in the sacriligious score of 121 strokes, and so the first four holes were promptly reduced to two, which in turn reduced the overall total to eighteen, the standard to which all other golf courses in the world aspired.

While the Old Course is the living heart of St Andrews, it is not the only relic of the town's golfing past. The graveyard of the ruined Cathedral is the last resting place of some of St Andrews most famous golfing sons including Tom Morris and Allan Robertson, and at Holy Trinity Church in the town there still remains the old 'Seat of Repentance' for those golfers who broke the law by playing golf on the Sabbath. Considered as most sinful in 1599, the next step on from public ridicule was excommunication!

Nowadays, even the town center itself has been taken over by the golfing industry. Shops selling clubs, balls, caps, jumpers, trousers, plus-fours; anything, no matter how trivial connected with the game, can be bought from one of the golfing stores that line St Andrews' historic high street. The annual turnover for shopkeepers is enormous.

Above: *The first Open Championship to be held at St Andrews was in 1873. Since then every great name in golf has opened their round in front of the imposing R & A clubhouse.*

St Andrews is also the home of the Royal and Ancient Golf Club. With golf thought to have been played at St Andrews since the early fifteenth century, the R&A is perhaps not quite as 'ancient' as it might first appear. The original club was formed in May 1754 by 'twenty-two Nobleman and Gentleman being admirers of the ancient and healthful exercise of the Golf'. Taking a lead from the Honourable Company at Leith, the original Society of St Andrews Golfers raised enough funds by 1754 to purchase their own silver club as a competition prize, in keeping with the élite tone of their rivals, the Honourable Company of Edinburgh Golfers. The Earl of Elgin and Lord Wemyss, along with 22 other founder members, helped to draft the first rules and conditions for

Below: *The Old Course at St Andrews: the scene of many professional tournaments over the past 150 years.*

the event. With the Leith code of rules accepted almost word for word, the event went ahead with merchant William Landale as the eventual winner. Landale was also given the privilege of being the first official Captain of the Society.

In 1835 the St Andrews Golfers moved from their private rooms at Ballie Glass's Inn into their new home at the Union Club directly opposite the links. A year before the move, the Society stole a march on their rivals at Leith by applying to King William IV to be renamed the Royal and Ancient Golf Club. This was granted, and two years later in 1837 the King William IV Gold Medal was inaugurated at the club's Autumn Meeting.

With the Honourable Company struggling at the overcrowded Leith links, the Royal and Ancient quietly established itself at the heart of golf, with golfers throughout Scotland referring to them on all matters concerning the rules. With a more permanent and prestigious home needed, the Royal and Ancient built its present clubhouse in 1854. Today, the club continues to be a world center of rule-making along with the United States Golf Association in America.

Apart from legislating on the rules of golf, perhaps the most important function of the Royal and Ancient is its supervision of the Open and Amateur Championships. Totally independent of the Professional Golfers' Association and European Tour, the R&A guides the development of both tournaments with experience born out of years of history and tradition.

Most books detailing the history of golf appear to show a rapid increase in popularity from the mid-eighteenth century onwards. A closer look, however, reveals a different story; it shows that within half a century of the first organized societies being formed, the game of golf had fallen into decline. In a crisis that would be unimaginable today, the great majority of Scottish golfers had turned their back on the game. Many ancient links, including the legendary Old Course at St Andrews, had been sold off for farming land and were in danger of being plowed up. By 1840, caddies stood idle on the links, while skilled club- and ball-makers had long since lost their livelihoods. Effectively, golf in Scotland, and therefore the world, seemed to have died!

So, how did this crisis arise? Before 1750, there was little sign of danger. Golf had been adopted as the national pastime of Scotland. The Honourable Company of Edinburgh Golfers had just been formed at Leith, and the game had just published its first official rules. Golf was still enjoyed by rich and poor alike, with links from St Andrews to Aberdeen being crowded with eager converts to the game. But after 14 July 1789 all this was to change.

With the storming of the Bastille in Paris, the French Revolution had lit a flame across Europe. The lower classes had risen up against their aristocratic masters and started a social revolution which engulfed the whole of Europe for the next four decades. In Scotland, as in England, the fear of invasion and a French-style revolution introduced social tensions. Public

demonstrations across the country were ruthlessly put down by the authorities. In Edinburgh, troops had opened fire on a crowd chanting Napoleonic slogans in an attempt to put down insurrection. Combined with economic pressures and fueled by higher prices for bread and ale, lower class resentment grew toward anything or anyone considered upper class – which in the later years of the eighteenth century included anyone who played golf.

Often abused in the streets, members of élite golf societies like the Honourable Company of Edinburgh Golfers were singled out. With the situation in Edinburgh becoming increasingly tense, the gentleman golfers began to avoid the public links like Leith and Bruntsfield. Denied the patronage of their wealthiest members, both courses quickly fell into disrepair, becoming overgrown and unusable. Away from Edinburgh, the situation at St Andrews was little better. With the town starved of money in 1797, St Andrews Council was forced to sell the land on which the Old Course stood. Under the conditions of sale, the golf links were thought to have been protected, but when the original buyer sold the lease to a third party who had no interest in golf, a massive legal battle commenced.

To the dismay of the few golfers who were left, the new owner established a large-scale rabbit breeding business on the links. Shortly after, the Old Course was extensively pitted with rabbit scrape and other hazards. The remaining members of the Society of St Andrews golfers took the matter all the way to the House of Lords. After a long legal battle, they finally established the ancient right of 'usage' over ownership, and won the case. The Lords of Appeal ruled that, as golf was known to have been played over the land for many centuries, it must have prior claim over any other use.

Another event which was to have profound effect on golf in the early nineteenth century was the systematic erosion of the ancient common land traditionally used for sport. With the onset of the Industrial Revolution, towns and cities across Scotland were expanding at an alarming rate. Increased building near 'town' courses like Leith in Edinburgh resulted in the five-hole links being closed in on all sides. Even at St Andrews the close proximity of the town to the first and eighteenth fairways shows

Far right: *Peter McEwan (1834-1895), named after his grandfather, continued the family clubmaking business at Musselburgh.*

Left: *The grave of Allan Robertson, situated amongst the ruins of St Andrews cathedral.*

how close golf came to losing two of its most celebrated holes. With the rapid decline in golf, the pressure to make better use of the land was intense – if not for building, then for growing wheat. Because of crop shortages in the proceeding years, wheat was fetching high prices in the late 1790s and was the main reason why so many early courses were plowed under for farm land.

To compound matters, a serious period of inflation in the early 1820s had a devastating effect on the finances of many Scottish institutions. The Honourable Company of Edinburgh Golfers was among the first to suffer. In slightly better financial shape than their rivals at St Andrews, they had raised a bank loan of £500 in 1824 to build their new golf house at Leith. Four years later another £200 was needed, and the interest on the debt began to mount up. By 1834 they were forced to sell the club and everything in it just to avoid bankruptcy. The Thistle Golf Club, who also played over Leith links, failed to outlast the crisis and disbanded during the late 1820s.

The difficulties at Leith were mirrored elsewhere in Scotland. By 1830, the Glasgow Golf Club was disbanded, as was the prestigious Kingsbarn Club between St Andrews and Crail. Aberdeen in the north remained neglected for many years, with only the faithful club secretary turning up for the annual general meeting. In Dunbar golfers were driven from the links and the land sold off to pay for a new harbour. Scotscraig Golf Club was plowed under for farming land in 1834, while golfers at Montrose and Elie had to petition the County Sheriff to stop their landlord from doing exactly the same.

A declining membership and lack of funds meant that even North Berwick suffered the indignity of giving up the links on Saturdays to allow local fishermen to dry their nets.

By 1840 golf had all but died out in Scotland, with many of the great links lying empty and overgrown. Abandoned by the moneyed classes and out of favor with the ordinary Scottish people, golf was in terminal decline. Even in England, Royal Blackheath was finding things difficult without the financial input of its Scottish members, while the Old Manchester Golf Club, was on the brink of liquidation.

How the game of golf pulled itself back from the brink of extinction has always been a matter for debate. Essentially, the times themselves changed. The industrial and social revolutions which threatened the very survival of golf ultimately became its savior. The wealth generated by new industry put money in the pockets of those who previously had none and golf slowly began to find favor with general Scottish Society. In the decades immediately following the introduction of the cheaper guttie ball in 1848 the game of golf came within reach of the pockets of increasing numbers of ordinary citizens.

In 1851 there were just 24 golf clubs in the whole of Great Britain. Less than half a century later, in 1899, there were 1,276. This rapid growth illustrates just how much the game was eventually to recover. However, this dark period in the history of golf was not without some casualties. Many early Scottish clubs like East Lothian, Collingsburgh and Kingsbarn were all disbanded and never reformed. The ancient Leith links – original home of the Honourable Company - fell into disrepair in the 1880s and sadly no longer exists. Bruntsfield, the favored golf course of Scottish kings in the late sixteenth century, survives today as a shabby pitch and putt course under the shadow of Edinburgh Castle.

Thankfully, other Scottish links were more fortunate; the Crail Golfing Society was dissolved in 1813 only to be resurrected many years later, while other great Scottish treasures like St Andrews, Montrose, Musselburgh and Aberdeen all managed to survive by the skin of their golfing teeth. The 'Golf Crisis' of the early nineteenth century is all but forgotten, but while it lasted it threatened the very survival of the game we enjoy today.

*A Victorian golfing scene at North Berwick, West Course. In the background is Bass Rock.*

The first British Open Championship was held in October 1860 at Prestwick Golf Club in Ayr, Scotland. Compared with the multimillion pound sporting event of today, this was a relatively modest affair with only eight professionals and absolutely no prize money to be won. Although not truly open until the following year when amateurs were allowed to enter, it became commonly known throughout the golfing world as the Open Championship.

Before the first championship got underway on 17 October 1860, an argument had long raged in Scotland about who was the country's finest golfer. The popular choice of most people was Allan Robertson. A feather ball-maker by trade, Robertson was renowned for being the only man to ever break 80 on the Old Course at St Andrews. Considered a miraculous score at the time, it was during a period when scratch amateurs were winning R&A Medal competitions with gross scores of 98 or more. Reputed never to have lost a singles match on level terms, Roberton's reputation for dogged determination was unsurpassed.

The man most favored to take his crown was his onetime apprentice, Tom Morris. A former St Andrews man himself, Morris had clashed bitterly with Robertson over the new guttie ball introduced in 1848, and Morris left St Andrews in 1853 to take up a new position as 'Keeper of the Greens' at Prestwick.

In the following years both men played a series of big money challenge matches against other professionals like Willie Park and Andrew Strath, but never against each other. With Morris's reputation growing ever stronger, his supporters openly accused Robertson of avoiding his younger rival. A proud and stubborn man, Robertson steadfastly refused to play in any match, singles or doubles, that included Tom Morris.

In 1855 Prestwick Golf Club proposed a championship finally to settle the issue. Aware that neither man could resist the chance to become the Scottish Champion, they proposed that St Andrews should be the venue for the first tournament. Despite pressure from Prestwick for an answer, St Andrews continued to procrastinate, so an approach was made to Musselburgh, but they also failed to reply. Then tragically Allan Robertson succumbed to an attack of jaundice which ended his life in 1859. Frustrated at the turn of events, and upset by their treatment from the more senior clubs, Prestwick pushed ahead to hold its own championship in 1860.

Each club in Scotland was invited to send its professional to compete for the title 'Champion Golfer.' With the Ayrshire coast being a long and difficult journey from Edinburgh and St Andrews, the first championship had an entry of just eight professionals. Apart from Tom Morris and Willie Park (Musselburgh's champion), entries were accepted from Andrew Strath, Charles Hunter, Alexander Smith, William Steel and Bob Andrew (nicknamed 'The Rook'). Although no prize money was on offer a champion's belt was to be given to the person who won the event three years in succession. The belt, similar to those awarded to the champion prize-fighters of the time, was subscribed to by every club member. An elaborate combination of red Moroccan leather and inscribed silver panels, it was commissioned at the not inconsiderable cost of 30 guineas.

Prior to 1860, organized tournaments like the one planned for Prestwick were not particularly popular with golf professionals. Despite the opportunity of winning the belt at some point in the future, many of them had little interest in competing for glory alone. With the exception of Tom Morris, the majority of early professionals scratched a living by caddying and teaching a few lessons. Occasionally they would play in individual or foursome challenge matches which enabled wealthy amateurs to wager large sums on the outcome. With a small percentage of the pot going to the professional taking part, it proved a lucrative way of supplementing a fairly meager existence.

Shortly before the 'official' tournament began,

Left: *Andrew Strath, winner of the Open Championship in 1865.*

Above: *The Earl of Eglington who helped establish the first Open Championship in 1860, played at Prestwick.*

Prestwick received a request from Royal Blackheath in London asking to enter their professional, George Daniel Brown. Major Fairlie, the Prestwick member who had first proposed the tournament, granted the request on the grounds that, as G. D. Brown was a Scot, it should not be held against him that he had chosen to work in England.

During the practice rounds, onlookers appeared to be alarmed at the professionals' generally scruffy appearance. It was even rumored that one of the competitors had spent the night in the local prison on a charge of drunkenness. With the possibility that women might be watching, it was decided by the committee that a suit of clothing would be given to every competitor to spare any unnecessary blushes. So it was that on the day every professional who played in the first Open Championship was dressed identically in the Earl of Eglington's green tartan.

The first Open Championship got underway with a sizeable gallery. In 1860, Prestwick was a 3,799 yard twelve-hole course, and it was decided that the tournament should be played over three 'rounds', with the lowest score as the winner. Despite it being the first time that these great players had come together, it was considered nothing more than a local Prestwick affair by St Andrews and Musselburgh. With little public interest, only one local newspaper – the *Ayr Advertiser* – chose to

cover the event. The play was described thus:

'A great match of golf was played yesterday, and excited the ambition of the crack players in the land ... The game made much progress, and became evident to the various tyrol that the tug of war would be between the champions of Prestwick (Morris) and Musselburgh (Park). Morris was the favourite as much on the account of his deservedly great reputation as much as the advantage he enjoyed traversing his own ground. At first however, this pleasing anticipation was dashed by the extraordinary good fortune of Park.'

In the first round, Tom Morris played in the group just ahead of his rival, Willie Park. On the opening day, Morris scored 58 to find himself trailing by three shots to Park's fine round of 55. The *Ayr Advertiser* noted how disappointed Morris's supporters were, and how they were 'buoying themselves on hope of him recovering himself in the second round'.

Sadly for Tom Morris, his second round 59 only matched that of Willie Park. In the third and final round both men battled it out over the final twelve holes. With no more than four shots ever separating them, Park eventually came to the last hole needing two putts from ten yards to win by a shot. To the despair of Tom Morris and his supporters, Willie Park holed out to win by two. Despite the local man losing, the Ayr reporter was generous in his praise for the overall standard of play. He wrote: 'We have no hesitation in saying, that at times the game of golf was never seen in such great perfection.' Apart from the shock defeat of Tom Morris, the Prestwick Club was delighted with the way the tournament had been received. After presenting Willie Park with the Championship belt, it announced the next tournament would be 'open to the world'.

History records that the first eleven Open Championships were held at Prestwick. Despite opening up the tournament to

Left: *Willie Park Snr, who beat 'Old' Tom Morris by two strokes to win the first Open Championship.*

amateurs in 1861, the entries continued to range between eight and seventeen. After Willie Park's momentous victory, the next decade was dominated by Tom Morris – Senior and Junior. Of the eleven Open Championships played between 1861 and 1872, the Morrises won eight titles between them – Tom Morris Snr in 1861–62–64–67 – and Tom Morris Jnr in 1868–69–70–72. It is likely that 'young' Tom would have made it five consecutive titles had he played in 1871 but, having already been presented with the Championship Belt for winning three times running, the embarrassed Prestwick club cancelled the following year's tournament because they had not organized a trophy in time.

This oversight caused the whole Open Championship system to be reviewed. Despite being the driving force behind these early tournaments, Prestwick had never wanted to be the only venue for the Open. Thankfully, the drama of the early Opens had caused widespread interest throughout Scotland, and it was decided that Prestwick, St Andrews and Musselburgh should hold the competition in turn. This three-course rota system stayed in place until 1892 when Musselburgh was replaced by Muirfield.

Tom Morris Jnr's fourth Open victory in 1872 was the first occasion the present silver claret jug was played for. However, unlike the Championship belt, Prestwick Golf Club sensibly declined to let it become the property of any future three-time winner. Perhaps it was understandable: 'Young' Tom was the dominant player of the time – and still only twenty-one! His greatest rival was his father and even 'Old' Tom himself later admitted, 'I could cope wi' Allan [Robertson] myself, but never wi' Tommy.'

Tom Morris Jnr was just thirteen when he attempted to enter his first professional tournament at Perth. The officials insisted he was too young, but arranged for him to play against another outstanding local boy, Willie Greig. A five-pound wager was placed on the match which Tom took with ease. His performance in beating Greig that day had impressed everyone and he was openly referred to as a future champion golfer.

After the match with Greig, Young Tom Morris's career began to take off. Three years later, aged sixteen, he amazed everyone by defeating top professionals Bob Andrews and Willie Park in a play-off at Carnoustie. In 1867 he competed in his first Open Championship and finished a creditable fourth behind his father in first place. The following year he won himself, playing three rounds at Prestwick in a record score of 154. Together with scooping the winner's prize money of £6, his victory heralded a period of unrivalled domination.

In 1869 he beat runner-up Bob Kirk by a clear margin of eleven strokes to record his second win. Then just in case Bob Kirk had any other ideas, Young Tom extended the winning margin over him to twelve shots in the following year. Aged just nineteen, Tom Morris Jnr had won his third consecutive Open title, and was presented with the Championship Belt for him to keep forever. Coming into his physical prime, he recorded his fourth victory in 1872 and was considered by those who played him, including his father, to be almost unbeatable.

Broad-shouldered, and with a perfect putting touch, Young Tom was at the pinnacle of his playing career by 1873. Simply too good for the opposition, he started looking for more unusual golfing challenges. In one particular match, he beat the better-ball scores of Jamie Anderson and Davie Strath. Despite finishing runner-up in 1873 to Tom Kidd and in 1874 to Mungo Park, it looked increasingly likely that he would go on to win more Open titles, but tragically this was not to be the case.

Young Tom Morris's last important match took place at North Berwick in September 1875. He and his father had been challenged by brothers, Willie and Mungo Park to a much publicized

*Right: 'Young' Tom Morris proudly wearing the Open Championship belt. After winning it three years in succession (1868-1870) it became his own property.*

challenge match. After winning on the final hole, Young Tom was handed a telegram informing him that his wife had been taken seriously ill while giving birth to their first child. It was decided to cut the journey in half by traveling across the Firth of Forth, but while the boat was made ready a second message arrived. Passed to Old Tom, it gave the tragic news that both mother and baby had died. In what must have been a distressing journey for the father, he chose not to tell his son until they had arrived back in St Andrews. After docking in the harbor, Dr Boyd who had attended Tom's wife, went down to meet them. He later described how after being given the news by his father, Young Tom kept crying, 'It's not true. It's not true...'. 'I have seen many sorrowful things,' reported the Doctor, 'but not many like that Saturday night.'

From that moment on, Tom Morris Jnr lost interest in everything, including golf. His friends and family rallied around but nothing could be done to bring him out of his melancholy. Then, curiously, he was persuaded to play in a challenge match against Arthur Molesworth, a well-known amateur player from Royal North Devon. In an ill-considered act of bravado, Molesworth had let it be known that upon receipt of a 'third' (six-strokes over eighteen holes), he would play any professional in Scotland for money.

The match was set for November and it was played over the Old Course at St Andrews. Quite why Young Tom took the challenge is uncertain, but those who watched the match reported the disinterested way that he tackled the match. Competing against the English amateur for three days, two rounds a day, Morris was clearly in command. Despite the Scottish weather being bitterly cold with snow and ice scattered across the Old Course, Molesworth refused to stop. Cold and undernourished, Young Tom still beat him nine and seven, and took the prize money on offer, but sadly, the true cost of the game was to prove far greater than anyone expected. Exhausted by the strain of the match and everything that had gone before, he retired to his bed. Shortly afterwards, on Christmas Day 1875, Young Tom Morris was found dead in his room. He was 24 years old.

Tom Morris Jnr was buried in the cemetery of the ruined Cathedral at St Andrews with his beloved wife and child. As proof of his popularity, 60 golfing societies contributed toward a memorial in his honor. Today his grave, with its white stone image of Young Tom ready to play an iron shot, is visited by golfing pilgrims from all over the world. After the death of his son, Old Tom never played the Open again – preferring instead to concentrate on his club-making business in St Andrews. In May 1908, Tom Morris Snr fell down the stairs of the Union Club at St Andrews and died shortly afterwards. He was 87 and had survived two of his sons and one daughter.

In honor of his memory, no golf was played at St Andrews on the day of his funeral. Thousands lined the streets to pay their last respects, including hundreds of children who had been given the day off school. Buried close to his beloved Young Tom, his final resting place is only a long putt away from his own boyhood rival, Allan Robertson. Not long before his death, Old Tom had watched from his chair on the first tee at St Andrews as the new generation of golfing greats paraded before him. Vardon, Braid and Taylor had all played Open Championships on the Old Course before 1908. As he watched them tee-off how his thoughts must have been drawn back to those early years at Prestwick.

Today at St Andrews the image of Old Tom Morris continues to look down onto the first tee on the Old Course. In honor of the 'Grand Old Man of Golf' his bust was inserted into the front of the Royal and Ancient clubhouse. Now inextricably linked, the legend of Old and Young Tom Morris will live on as long as the Open Championship is played.

Below: *Prestwick Golf Club, original home to the British Open Championship.*

During the reign of Queen Victoria, golf evolved from an exclusively Scottish pastime to a pre-eminent sport played in every far-flung corner of the British Empire. From Musselburgh to Montreal, St Andrews to Sydney, and Blackheath to Bombay, golf was truly a game on which the sun never set. Many theories have been offered which explain why golf became so popular in such a short space of time – the introduction of the guttie ball; cheaper mass-produced golf equipment; the expansion of the railways – all these elements are valid and important and are dealt with in due course. The more accurate explanation, however, is that golf's rapid growth was due to the much larger social change which took place in Britain in the latter half of the nineteenth century. A time of progress, innovation and of course the Industrial Revolution, this period can be described as the 'Golden Age of Golf'.

By the end of the nineteenth century, Victorian Britain had come to symbolize progress and expansion. In a period of unprecedented growth, England mined more than half the world's coal; manufactured more pig-iron than the United States, Germany and Russia put together; and manufactured three-quarters of the world's cotton. The British Empire which covered a quarter of the earth's surface, led the world in

Above: *Gibsons of Kinghorn, were amongst the first club makers to mass produce sets of iron-headed clubs.*

areas of finance, medicine and education, and was the greatest single influence on world affairs.

It was also a time of unprecedented growth for the game of

Left: *It was during the late Victorian era that the popularity of golf spread far beyond British shores. This photograph shows golfers in Ceylon at the turn of the century.*

Above: *Tom Williamson, professional at Nottingham Golf Club, with his staff in 1900. Note the wooden shafted clubs at the side.*

golf. Beginning in 1848 with introduction of the guttie ball, the popularity of golf quickly became more widespread. Because it was less than one-quarter the price of the old feather ball, working-class could people look at golf as an alternative to other sports. Horace Huchinson wrote in *Golf* magazine in 1897 that, 'with the introduction of the guttie ball, a comparative durable article at a shilling or nine pence, the game was at once brought within the means of many'. Hutchinson was proved right but it was by no means an instant transition. Perhaps even more than

cost, it was the availability of the new ball which made the difference. By the time Hutchinson made his comments, gutties were being produced in greater numbers than ever before and factory-based companies like Silvertown and Spalding produced literally thousands every week.

With cheap cost and availability contributing greatly to the success of the guttie ball, the same two factors applied equally to the manufacture of golf clubs. Like the feather ball, long-nose woods of the early nineteenth century were often hand-crafted to

Above: *The finishing shop at Gibsons of Kinghorn in 1896. After the iron heads came out of the forge, it was the job of these men to file, polish and stamp them in preparation for fitting with a hickory shaft.*

Right: *A lithographic poster extolling the virtues of playing golf at North Berwick in the early 1900s.*

individual order. The introduction of the hard guttie ball revolutionized club design almost overnight. The long slender shape of the early woods was replaced by thicker, more shock-absorbent heads. Another visible change was the greater amount of iron clubs being produced. Less prone to breaking than their wooden counterparts, they benefited from the great strides made in metal manufacture in the later years of the Industrial Revolution. Pioneered by progressive club-makers like Tom Stewart and Robert Forgan, the first sets of iron-headed clubs were mass-produced in the late 1890s

to cater for the increasing demand. With the cheaper price of equipment and the subsequent increase in golf courses, it was estimated that over £2,600,000 was spent on golf in 1899 alone.

Another factor contributing to the golfing boom was the growth of railways. Considered the most visible sign of progress, the Liverpool and Manchester Railway opened its first route in 1830 and within 25 years it had completely revolutionized English life and commerce. Before the railways, all transportation between major cities had been by canals and horse-drawn carriage, and

Above: *Golfing parlor games were increasingly popular in the late Victorian era.*

the journeys were often long, unpleasant and dangerous. With Britain linked by over 15,000 miles of track by 1870, the railways had the dual benefit of being cheap to travel on as well as enabling British industry to transport its goods more quickly and efficiently than ever before. The main line routes in place, the railways then spread to smaller areas, adding hundreds of new branch lines by 1880.

After the North British Railway Company extended a branch line from Leuchars to St Andrews in 1852, the old town experienced a boom of its own. Now within easy reach of Edinburgh

and even further afield, St Andrews attracted increasing numbers of visitors to play golf and enjoy the sights. Lack of accommodation was a problem at first but with money flowing into the town, hotels were soon built to satisfy demand. After the lean years of the early nineteenth century, the railway provided a welcome stimulus for many other Scottish golf resorts including Troon, Prestwick, Carnoustie and Aberdeen.

Further south in England, the expanding rail system and increased prosperity brought about by the Industrial Revolution was having a similar effect. With Victorian seaside resorts like Blackpool now accessible by rail, and cheap travel available to and from major cities like Birmingham and Manchester, new public golf courses were springing up in these areas. In May 1900, the *Blackpool Herald* carried a report on the positive economic effect which golf's popularity had achieved in the area: 'Golf has not only built hotels or enabled them to be built, but it has built boarding houses and club houses and made them into paying concerns ... Golf has made St Annes; it is now making Fairhaven.' Perhaps it would not be too strong a statement to say that if it was almost golf that made St Annes, then almost certainly Victorian England made golf the popular sport that it is today.

Below: *A scene from Royal St Davids in 1896 – playing golf in the shadow of Harlech castle.*

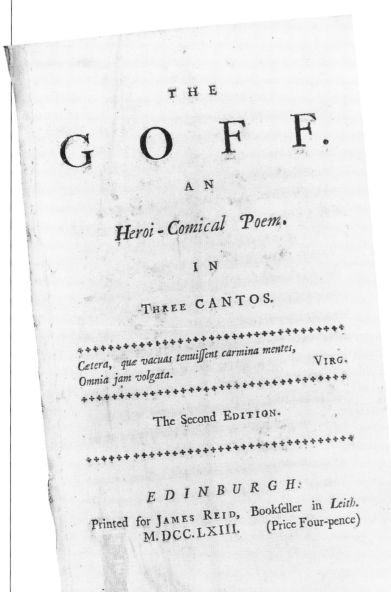

At the onset of the Industrial Revolution, Scottish firms were looking to expand south of the border. Manchester, second only to London in size and importance, was the obvious choice. A golf course was established in 1818, on the heathland slopes of Kersall Edge, north of the city. Second only in age to Royal Blackheath, which was established in 1787, the Old Manchester Golf Club was originally formed by Scottish business men living and working in Manchester but was used by few others. Golf was still an exclusively Scottish pastime in the early nineteenth century, with little English interest being shown in the game.

Before the Industrial Revolution a few expatriate Scotsmen had attempted to establish the game in England. After all, the first golf links on Blackheath had been marked out by the Scottish-born King James I for his own pleasure. In recent years, evidence has been unearthed about a hitherto unknown golf course in Brighton founded by Scotsmen. In a 1793 copy of Thomas Mathison's famous poem 'The Goff', a four-line handwritten note was found on the fly-leaf which read:

> 'From London some sons of Auld Reekie set forth
> To establish at Brighton a wee club of goff;
> The green at Blackheath is indeed very fair,
> But Blackheath and Brighton can never compare.'

Left: *The Goff* by Thomas Mathison – a 24-page leaflet published in 1743, it remains the earliest publication devoted entirely to the game of golf.

Left: *Originally an old tin hut, the clubhouse at Royal North Devon today, by the 18th hole.*

Below left: *The golfers here are gathering for a competition. Before clubhouse accommodation became more sophisticated, simple metal* constructions *were the norm, some even prefabricated by the manufacturers.* Above: *Mixed golf at Westward Ho! in 1902.*

The note, with its archaic spelling, offers likely proof that 'sons of Auld Reekie' (Glasgow) established the first golf course in the south of England. Another early English course which failed to survive was the ancient links at Molesey Hurst on the Surrey bank of the Thames, near Hampton Court. These were thought to be links where Catherine of Aragon played golf in 1513, and they were still going strong in 1758, when the Reverend Jupiter Carlyle described the course at Molesey Hurst as 'very good'. Sadly this historic course no longer exists despite being in constant use for almost two centuries. Like so many others, it waned in popularity as interest in the sport died out.

On the basis that neither Old Manchester nor Royal Blackheath now play on their original links, the Royal North Devon at Westward Ho has a valid claim to the title of 'first' English Golf Club. Formed in 1864 as the 'North Devon and West of England Golf Club' it remains the oldest private club in

*Above: A L.N.E.R poster showing the pleasures to be had playing golf at Cruden Bay in the early 1920s. Displayed at railway stations throughout Britain, it typifies the healthy outdoor image golf had at the time.*

England to still use its original course. Changed to Royal North Devon in 1867 after the Prince of Wales became its patron, the golf links at Northam Burrows still comprise much as the original course.

The early development of Royal North Devon was typical of what was later to become a common process in Victorian England: the first 'clubhouse' was nothing more than a mobile bathers' changing-room. On competition days it was stocked with food and drinks and physically dragged to the course by the members. This was replaced in turn by a bell-tent, a marquee and a small wooden hut with corrugated tin roof. During these early years, everything about the club was rough and ready; the wooden hut was only big enough to accommodate an old table, chairs and small bar, while the members' hickory clubs were placed upon the rafters for safe-keeping.

Situated near the first tee of the golf course, the 'clubhouse' soon attracted the unwelcome attention of local cattle farmers. In a situation that was to repeat itself all over England in the next 50 years, these 'pot-wallopers', as they were labelled by the members, bitterly resented the intrusion of golfers on common grazing land. Consequently, a war of attrition began which saw the hut being constantly vandalized, together with the golf course. The members' hut was finally relocated closer to the beach , but unfortunately things were little better there. With every new tide the hut was flooded and during the occasional Atlantic storm it was almost carried away.

Twenty years after the Royal North Devon was formed, an uneasy truce between the golfers and pot-wallopers resulted in the building of a permanent new clubhouse. Built in 1887 for £800, it was made primarily of wood. It included two changing-rooms, a members' bar and a committee room – not surprisingly, it was welcomed by the members as 'a thing of beauty and a joy forever'.

Despite the progress made by the Royal North Devon Club in the mid-nineteenth century, English golf was still struggling to establish itself. The London Scottish Rifle Club – formed out of a Scottish Army regiment – had played golf over Wimbledon Common since 1862. Three years later they formed the London Scottish Golf Club, offering as a gesture of goodwill membership to any local English golfers. In honor of their military heritage, each member was asked to wear crimson to identify himself from other users of the common. Sixteen years later in 1881, a bitter rift developed with the club's English members which led to the Scottish Golfers leaving to form their own club on the opposite side of Wimbledon Common. Today the two golf clubs – London Scottish and Wimbledon Park – continue to use the same delightful links, but play it from opposite ends. Interestingly, the honor board at each club claims Club Captains dating back to 1865, while the tradition of always wearing crimson continues to this day.

Although golf was thought to have been played on open spaces throughout the capital, London Scottish and Royal Blackheath remained the only official clubs until the foundation of Clapham Common in 1873. A decade later, the British Government enacted part of its social legislation which made vast areas of common land across London open for recreational purposes. Almost immediately, common land at Tooting Bec, Epsom and Epping Forest were all utilized for golf. Before moving to Deal in 1890, the original Prince's Golf Club played over Mitcham Common, while at the same time Thames Ditton and Esher established a short nine-hole course on Esher Common. Despite the high cost of building golf courses in the London area, the number of clubs grew from just six in 1899 to over 50 ten years later.

Despite the death of Queen Victoria in 1901, the popularity of golf continued during the next decade. From 1902 to 1905, the game received enthusiastic support from the Prime Minister, Arthur Balfour. A keen disciple, his attitude to golf was summed up in 1902 when he said, 'More and more people are beginning to discover that there is no better way of spending a holiday, no more reasonable or less elaborate method of enjoying a day's outing, than playing golf on a good links.'

Although golf was already popular in the early 1900s, it was the regular sight of Balfour on the links which ultimately made it fashionable. With decorative items proving increasingly popular, artists, sculptors, silversmiths and makers of ceramics all turned their hand to works of golfing interest. In a period where healthy exercise was considered paramount to achieving a healthy mind, the game of golf portrayed the image of fresh air, good exercise and well-mannered behavior. Introduced into all the leading public schools in the land, it became a necessary part of every young student's education. In a curious turnaround, after arriving from Scotland only 70 years before, golf was now considered the very epitome of 'English' sport.

In the years leading up to the start of World War I, golf's popularity suffered a setback. Arthur Balfour had retired and Britain was gripped by a new cynicism which left sport taking second place behind the more pressing realities of the time. But although golf was standing still in Britain, it was thriving throughout the rest of the Empire, and was undergoing a boom of its own in the United States, where it had been played since 1888. While the early years of American golf are dealt with in greater detail in Chapter Eighteen, it is time to see how golf spread outside Britain throughout the rest of the world.

Left: *Arthur Balfour*

RULE X
Any vessel or similar obstruction may be removed.

RULE XVII
Any loose impediments may be removed from the putting-green.

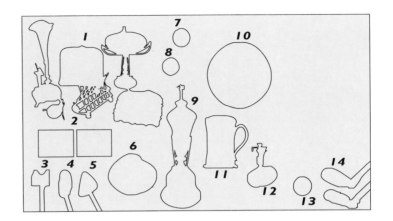

1  *A selection of golfing silverware from 1905.*  2  *Two plates from the* Perrier Rules of Golf *book illustrated by Chas Crombie. Original edition 1900.*  3  *An illegal mallet-head putter – stymie lofter, 1910.*
4  *Spalding Schenectady putter.*  5  *Patent putter.*  6  *Coffee cup and saucer, Stafford china, 1905.*  7  *Arch Colonel golf ball, 1908.*
8  *Midge golf ball, 1910.*  9  *Silver trophy supported by four golf clubs, 1920.*  10  *Decorated china plate by Grimwades, 1908.*
11  *Royal Doulton jug decorated with white relief panels of golfers, 1910.*  12  *Brass radiator cap mascot, 1915.*  13  *Bramble golf ball, 1905.*  14  *Urquhart No 2698 adjustable golf club, 1900.*

Above: *An international club match between Royal Montreal and Brookline Country Club in 1898. This type of inter-club match became increasingly popular as golf began to grow in America during the 1900s.*

In 1829 India was the first established outpost of the British Empire. Golf was originally introduced into the Indian sub-continent by soldiers, settlers and government administrators. The Royal Bombay Golf Club was founded in 1842, and was known to have presented a silver medal to the Royal and Ancient Golf Club in 1845. However, the oldest golf club in India is thought to be the Royal Calcutta. The club records date back to 1876, when golf was first introduced into the area around Dum-Dum (where Calcutta International airport is situated today) by the East India Company around 1830. The oldest established golf clubs outside the British Isles, Bombay and Calcutta are second only in age to the early Scottish clubs.

Around the same time as Royal Bombay was becoming established, golf had just taken its first faltering steps in the new world. Unlike India, with its strong British influence, golf was introduced into North America by Scottish settlers in the mid-nineteenth century. Through newspaper reports of the time, we know that golf was played in America between 1795 and 1830. Played by early Scottish settlers in Charleston, South Carolina and Savannah, Georgia, it appeared to fade away in the early 1800s.

Further north in Canada, sporadic attempts to start the game around Quebec were reported as early as 1824. Almost 50 years on in 1873, a small band of Scots came together to form the

Montreal Golf Club. The driving force behind the project was Alexander Dennistoun – 'The father of Canadian Golf'. Two years later, the Quebec Golf Club finally sparked into life. Second only to Royal Montreal in age, its early years were helped by the able advice of Old Tom Morris's sister, who had married and was living there.

During the mid-nineteenth century, golf was also being played in Argentina by exiled Scots working on the railways. As in Britain, the Argentinian government had invested a fortune in laying down railway lines across the country. In a twenty-year period from 1860 to 1880, experienced British workers were brought over to help supervise and lay the thousands of miles

Below: 'Crossing Jordan' by Garden Grant Smith, RSW. This painting of Pau Golf Club was completed in 1892.

of tracks. With many Scots among them, it was only a matter of time before golf started to be played. In 1878, the Buenos Aires Golf Club was formed, followed twelve years later by the São Paulo club in Brazil.

Three decades after becoming established in India, the game of golf had spread to the rest of Asia. In the short time between 1888 and 1891, courses were instigated by British expatriates in Bangkok, Singapore, Hong Kong and Taiping in Malaya. In Australia, golf was played in Melbourne as early as the 1840s. A short-lived affair, it was formally ended with a dinner at the Royal Oak Hotel in 1850. The present-day Royal Melbourne Golf Club – home to many professional championships – was not revived until 1891. Despite Melbourne's claim to be the first place in Australia where golf was played, the title of oldest club officially belongs to Royal Adelaide. This club started with a small nine-hole layout in 1870, and the Governor of the colony, Sir James Ferguson, was known to have provided the first clubs and balls. Probably providing-nothing more than a casual knock-about for fellow officers, the 'club' disbanded soon after Ferguson's departure in 1873. The present Royal Adelaide Golf Club was reconstituted on 11 August 1892, moving to its present course at Seaton twelve

years later. The late nineteenth century saw the birth of many of Australia's finest golf clubs, all of which survive today. They include Royal Queensland (1890), Royal Sydney (1893), Royal Perth (1895), and Royal Hobart (1900).

Another great outpost of the British Empire at the turn of the century was South Africa. Royal Cape was the first golf club, established on the African continent in 1885, in the same year as General Sir Henry Torrens was sent to command the British troops at the Cape of Good Hope. Within days of his arrival he had marked out a rudimentary nine-hole course near Wynberg Barracks on Waterloo Green. Six years later, the Club moved to Rondebosch Common, sharing it with Cape Town's rubbish tip and a Malay graveyard. As for Torrens, he left South Africa in 1888, moving on to become Governor of Malta where he immediately established the Royal Malta Golf Club.

Remaining on the African continent, golf was first introduced into Rhodesia (modern-day Zimbabwe) in 1895. Originally played at Bulawayo two years after the bloody Matebele War, it evolved into the Salisbury Golf Club in 1989 moving to its present-day site in 1901. Edward, Prince of Wales, was known to have played there in 1925. Four years later in 1929, King George V, perhaps on his son's advice,

Right: *Knocke Zoute Golf Club in Belgium. King Leopold III, a keen golfer himself, competed here in the Belgian Amateur Championship in 1939.*

Above: *A holiday postcard from the turn of the century depicting golfing in the Alps.*

granted the Royal title to Salisbury Golf Club, which was later changed to Royal Harare in 1983.

In Europe, as everywhere else in the world, golf was the main sporting pastime of the British. The first golf club founded on the Continent was the Pau Golf Club in France. A favorite playground of the rich and famous, golf was played there as early as 1856. The attractive parkland course was originally built by British expatriates in the shadow of the Pyrenees, where it quickly evolved into a long-stay resort for well-to-do holidaymakers.

Also established by British residents in 1888, Royal Antwerp is the oldest private golf club in Belgium. After moving from its original site in 1910, it maintained the British 'feel' of the club by employing Scottish golf architect, Willie Park Jnr, to design the new course at Kepellenbos just north of the city.

Soon after 1900, six other Belgian golf courses followed in quick succession, but for the first time in European history they were not instigated by the British – they were aimed, however,

at attracting British golfers. King Leopold II, realizing the importance of trading links with post-Victorian Britain, introduced more golf courses into his country to make the British feel more at home. This involved making land available for courses at Ostend and in the Royal parks outside Brussels. He also persuaded the Wagon-Lits company to build a golf course in the scenic grounds of Chateau Royal d'Ardenne at Dinant. All six private golf clubs that were set up during this period are still flourishing today.

By the advent of World War I, golf had spread across most of the world. The gradual process had taken the best part of 90 years, beginning with those early groups of Scottish pioneers who had carried their national pastime to all four corners of the globe. They had been followed in the mid-nineteenth century by the ever-expanding British Empire, and golf remains to this day an enormously popular sport enjoyed by thousands all over the world.

The Industrial Revolution, which had swept Victorian England, and its mercantile aftermath now turned its attention to the business of sport – and golf in particular. In the boom years from 1890 to 1914, literally hundreds of patents were taken out relating to golf. Prior to that date, only fourteen were registered with the London Patents Office. Now, most related to clubs and balls, but many more took in accessories like tees, golf bags and even collapsible flag-sticks.

Historically, the boom in patent applications from 1890 onwards coincided with the increasing popularity of golf in Britain and America. Doomed as many of those ideas were, they typify a time of tremendous optimism when the common feeling was that anything was possible. Unlike today, there were few regulations controlling the design of golf clubs and balls. Despite a powerful move to ban the innovative 'Haskell' rubber-core ball in the early 1900s, the size and weight of golf balls were not standardized until much later, while rules concerning golf club design only came in around 1908. Effectively, this gave free reign to the inventive Victorian mind to come up with ideas that would revolutionize the game.

With no restrictions on the shape, size or type of materials used in the making of the club-head, it is remarkable what ideas did actually surface. Some, like hippopotamus-faced woods (1899), were plainly bizarre, but others were astonishing in their futuristic insight; for example, Englishman William Mills patented the first metal-headed woods as early as 1896. To further emphasize the point, other innovations years ahead of their time included moulded plastic heads (1904), heel and toe weighting (1897), cavity-backed irons (1893), one-piece woods (1896), glass-headed putters (1908), adjustable irons (1892), and steel tees for frosted ground (1896).

Despite many of these ideas being in use today, it appears that none of the original inventors ever made their fortunes – indeed many lost money as they tried to put their ideas into production. Typical of these was the blacksmith from Edinburgh called Thomas Horsburgh who invented the first steel shaft in 1894. A scratch handicap player himself, he failed to persuade any of the local club-professionals to try them out. Whether it was lack of interest on their part, or that they considered the steel shafts as a threat to their own livelihood, we shall never

Above: *Introduced into Great Britain in 1901, the early Haskell balls were considered a novelty.*

Right: *Many claims were made about the new rubber-core ball, including that putting was made easier.*

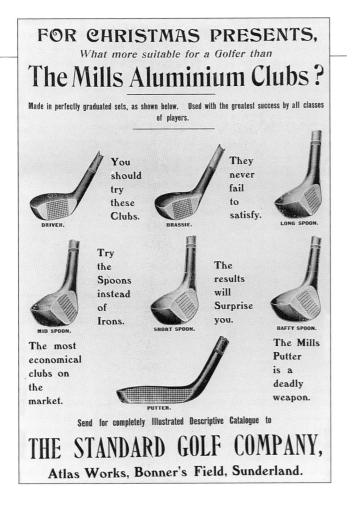

Above: *A selection of the aluminum clubs designed by Sir William Mills,
from driver to putter.*

know. After he had spent a small fortune developing the idea,
Horsburgh's steel shafts slowly died through lack of interest and
funds. Fortunately for Thomas Horsburgh and his family, his
later invention of the nailless horseshoe restored his finances
some years later.

Almost twenty years after Horsburgh's solid steel shaft, a
technical engineer called Saunders patented the first tubular
steel shaft. But even with the backing of the Accles & Pollock
Company – the leading golfing manufacturers of the time – the
concept was turned down by both the Royal and Ancient and the
United Stated Golfing Authority. With hickory still in worldwide use, it was thought the steel shafts would result in the ball
being hit too far. It seems unlikely today, but both ruling bodies
believed the increased cost to private golf clubs through having
to extend their golf courses as a result of the steel clubs would
bankrupt and kill off the game altogether. Eventually, in the

1920s, both organizations relented, but not until supplies of
hickory wood itself had run dangerously low and an alternative
had to be found.

This growing need for equipment legislation began as a
direct response to the introduction of the Haskell rubber-core
ball in 1902. Although more patents were taken out for the golf
ball than any other item of equipment from 1895 onwards, this
revolutionary new concept literally changed the face of golf for
decades to come, as well as instigating the most costly legal
battle in the history of the game.

In the late 1890s, American Coburn Haskell came upon the
idea of wrapping thin rubber strips around a central elastic core
under tension, then covering the whole thing with a gutta-percha shell. It was essentially the forerunner of the modern golf

Below: *Originally involved in the manufacture of bicycle tires, Coburn
Haskell of Cleveland, Ohio, went on to patent the first rubber-core golf
ball in 1898.*

Above: *With endorsements from James Braid and Harry Vardon, the Standard Golf Company went on to produce over 40 different types of aluminum putter and fairway club by 1914.*

ball. Haskell submitted the idea to the US patents office and went into golf ball production shortly after in 1898. Even with the 'old fashioned' gutta-percha cover, the ball was amazingly responsive and flew much farther than its predecessors, even when poorly struck. It was an incredible breakthrough which would ultimately signal the end of the solid guttie ball.

Named after its inventor, the Haskell's first success came in 1901 when Walter Travis used it to win the US Amateur Championship. A year later in England, Alex Herd was persuaded to try it during practice for the British Open Championship at Hoylake. He then went on to use the same ball for all four rounds, and won his one and only Open title. But there were those who regarded the new ball with contempt, believing it gave the users an unfair advantage. Old habits died hard and the ball was labeled

the 'Bounding Billy' because it continued to 'bound' along the fairway even when poorly struck (the name 'bounder' stuck for anyone who sought an unfair advantage).

By 1902, the Haskell ball had only achieved limited success in the USA. Manufactured by the Goodrich Tyre & Rubber Company of Akron, Ohio, they were more expensive than the guttie and in many cases less resilient. Despite Alex Herd's effort, they seldom lasted more than one round and proved difficult to control on or around the greens. Then, by mistake, a new 'bramble' pattern of reversed dimples was moulded onto a Haskell ball by professional David Foulis. The effect was immediate. The Haskell, which had been previously marked with the meshed lines of the old gutta, flew far better and was more controllable on the greens.

Based on Coburn Haskell's original design, a number of British golf ball manufacturers like Silvertown and St Mungo of Glasgow all took out licences to manufacture the new ball. Almost immediately there were patent infringements by other British companies eager to produce their own rubber-core ball. Haskell was forced to take the matter to court and in the most celebrated legal case of the time, the court moved against Hutchinson Main & Co of Glasgow, makers of the Springvale range of rubber-core balls.

Plainly Haskell should have won but, despite taking it to appeal at the House of Lords, the American inventor lost the case on the ruling of 'prior user'. Hutchinson Main had been able to prove that the idea of using wound rubber inside golf balls was not unknown in Britain prior to Haskell's patent of 1898. In a highly publicized court battle which had more than its share of anti-colonial feeling, various witnesses were produced to prove Hutchinson's case.

Haskell's loss meant that any ball manufacturer in Britain could now produce the rubber-cored balls. From 1902 to 1905, 97 golf ball patents were registered in Britain alone, and a further 41 in America – despite Haskell's patent still being in force over there. After the historic court ruling this number was to rise dramatically over the next few years, quickly followed by calls to

standardize the ball, perhaps even to ban its sale in Britain. But the cost and implications of the Haskell case had made everyone nervous, so the golfing authorities concentrated on the far safer area of golf clubs – a decision which was to cause yet another angry exchange with the Americans.

In 1908, the Rules of Golf Committee of the Royal and Ancient stated that any substantial departure from the traditional type of golf club would not be tolerated. A year later, a new croquet-style putter fell foul of the new ruling, with the ban extending to the popular American Schenectady putter. With tens of thousands of putters already in circulation in the United States, threats were made and a major crisis developed between the USGA and the R&A. Ultimately the R&A won out, even though the Americans continued to sanction the Schenectady. It was ruled from then onwards that any golf club not designed within strictly 'traditional' guidelines must first seek R&A approval before manufacture – a situation that still applies today.

With hindsight, the patent wars were to prove the first steps toward the mechanization and mass-production of golfing equipment that we have today. They also signaled the end of the maverick club-designer, who, with his weird and wonderful ideas, had communicated a small message of hope for the ordinary golfer.

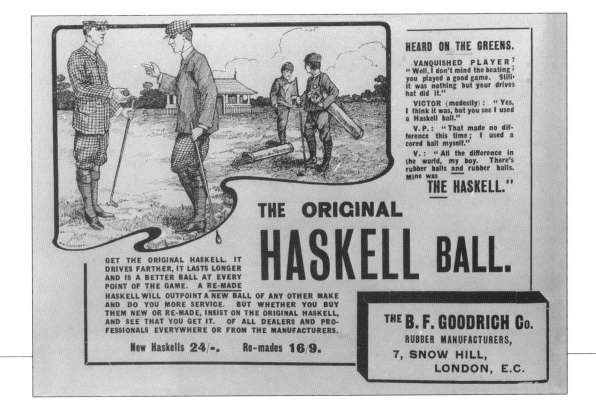

Left: *Originally the makers of the guttie ball, B. F. Goodrich & Co were the first manufacturers to produce the new Haskell rubber-core ball.*

In the 21 years before the outbreak of World War I, three men dominated the British Open Championship. Taking the title no fewer than sixteen times between them, Harry Vardon, James Braid and J. H. Taylor were acknowledged as the finest three professionals the world had ever seen. With each one a champion in his own right, they were know collectively as 'The Great Triumvirate'.

John Henry Taylor was the first English-born professional to win the Open Championship and the first of the Triumvirate to make a showing. His first victory at Sandwich in 1894 ended a Scottish dominance that stretched back to Willie Park in 1860. Born within chipping distance of Royal North Devon Golf Club on 19 March 1871, he was the son of a Northam laborer who had died while Taylor was still at school. Coming from a poor working-class background, Taylor helped to support his family by taking part-time jobs while still only young. It was while working as a house-boy at the home of the Hutchinson family that his interest in golf was sparked.

Horace Hutchinson, a top amateur of the time, would employ the young Taylor as his caddie. Taylor became hooked and soon

Above: *The Duke of York (later to become George V) hits the opening drive at Richmond Park Golf Club. He is watched by J. H. Taylor.*

Right: *From top left, clockwise: Alex Herd, J.H. Taylor, Harry Vardon and James Braid.*

started to emulate the style of local club professional Johnny Allan in his matches with the other caddies. In time, his flat-footed swing with its short punchy follow-through, was to become famous throughout the golfing world.

A scratch player by the time he was seventeen, he took a poorly paid pro-greenkeeper's post at Burnham and Berrow in 1891. A year later, he beat Andrew Kirkaldy in an exhibition match at the prestigious Winchester Golf Club, and was offered the job of club professional which he accepted. Buoyed-up by his performance against Kirkaldy, Taylor made his first appearance in the Open Championship at Prestwick in 1893. Because of his surprise victory over the experienced professional from St Andrews, other competitors lined up to play the young upstart. Typically, in the practice days that preceded the tournament, Taylor took them on one by one and beat all of them. Confident about his chances in the Open Championship itself, he opened with a course record score of 75. However, it was not to last; the strain of competing solidly day after day had taken its price, and Taylor stumbled badly in the following two rounds before finishing well down the list. Nevertheless, the Championship had been good experience which would serve him well in future Open Championships.

Despite winning the Open Championship in the following year, Taylor's golf game still had its critics. His winning score of 326 at Sandwich was abnormally high and there were some who felt that he was lucky to win. A deeply emotional man, he was obviously stung by the comments. Determined to prove them wrong, Taylor practiced relentlessly before the next year's Open on the Old Course at St Andrews. After playing well all week, Taylor beat Alex 'Sandy' Herd comfortably into second spot, making his a victory for determination as much as skill. On the strength of his victory at St Andrews, Taylor formed a club-making business with his lifelong friend George Cann. Soon after, he encountered the two men with whom his name would be permanently linked.

Above: *Five times Open champion J. H. Taylor.*
Below: *Edward, Prince of Wales, congratulates British Ryder Cup captain J. H. Taylor on his team's victory at Southport and Ainsdale.*

J. H. Taylor's first encounter with James Braid was in December 1895 at the West Drayton Golf Club. He had heard about the tall, silent Scot, but had never actually seen him play. Playing him in an exhibition match, the game ended closer than anyone had expected, with Braid holing a difficult putt on the 36th green to halve their game. Taylor deemed himself unlucky not to win, but he was under no such illusions against Harry Vardon at Ganton on 14 May 1896. Vardon destroyed him eight and seven, with Taylor commenting afterwards: 'I am not likely to forget it [the date] for the painful recollection that Vardon gave me of the biggest hiding I have ever received.' Over the next few years, Vardon's enormous talent was to deprive J. H. Taylor (among many others) of even more Open titles than the five he actually did win. But even with Vardon in the field, Taylor had won the British Open Championship in 1900, 1909 and 1913, as well as being runner-up in four straight years from 1904 to 1907.

Away from tournament play, Taylor continued to build up his increasingly successful club-mak-

ing and export business with George Cann. Despite his broadening financial interests in Britain and America, Taylor still enjoyed the relative security of the ordinary club professional's life. Having served his apprenticeship with Charles Gibson at Westward Ho!, Taylor enjoyed the daily contact with the members and discussing all aspects of golf. After spending six years at Winchester he moved to the prestigious Royal Wimbledon Golf Club in 1896, and then Royal Mid-Surrey three years later. Despite spending much of his time away playing tournaments and exhibition matches, Taylor always stayed true to his club roots.

Always concerned with raising the social standing of his fellow professionals, Taylor was not averse to using his famous name to call for improvements in wages and general working conditions. He was also instrumental in forming the first Professional Golfers Association in 1901.

Coming toward the end of his tournament playing career, Taylor played in his final Open Championship in 1926 at Royal Lytham St Annes – the same year which saw the first victory of the new generation of golfing champions in the shape of American Bobby Jones. While not performing well, it was still a fitting swan song for one of the greatest golfers who had ever lived. Retiring to the place of his birth John Henry Taylor died quietly in his small cottage looking over the Royal North Devon links aged 92.

Harry Vardon was born at Grouville, Jersey (Channel Islands), on 9 May 1970. Compared to Braid and Taylor, Vardon was a fluid, powerful player with a narrow stance and upright swing. Despite being dogged by ill-health and troubled by the putting 'yips' throughout his career, he is openly acknowledged as one of the greatest players of his generation. Six times British Open Champion, he was

*Left: The classic follow-through of Harry Vardon*

nicknamed 'the Stylist' by his fellow professionals for the graceful, easy way he played the game. He was also labeled 'the Greyhound' by Andrew Kirkaldy of St Andrews who, having seen Vardon overtake him so many times to win tournaments, was heard to mutter, 'Watch the Greyhound, watch the Greyhound!'

Having witnessed at first hand the rewards of the professional game from his elder brother, Tom, Harry left the Channel Islands aged just twenty to take up his first post at Lord Ripon's estate in Yorkshire. The course was a solitary nine-holer with few opportunities to play and practice, and Harry quickly moved on to a newly built golf course at Bury, but the rigors of a club professional's life were not to his liking, and he was desperate to test himself against the finest players available.

An early challenge match against Alex Herd of St Andrews offered a taste of what to expect. Defeated badly on that occasion, it made Vardon more determined than ever to prove himself. Entering his first British Open Championship at Prestwick in 1893, he finished a disappointing 22 shots behind the eventual winner Willie Auchterlonie. At St Andrews in the following year, Vardon led the first round only to finish in an eventual tie for ninth place. J. H. Taylor, who beat Alex Herd into second place that year, was strong favorite to make it three in a row at Muirfield in 1896. Playing at the top of his form, even Taylor himself was confident of victory, but he could not foresee the devastating effect that playing Harry Vardon earlier in the year would have on his game.

Vardon had just taken up his new post as club professional at Ganton in Yorkshire when an exhibition match was arranged with J. H. Taylor for the spring. Vardon was still a virtual unknown in 1896, but performed brilliantly on the day, easily defeating the current Open Champion. A humiliated Taylor later revealed how Vardon's exceptional play that day had shaken him for the rest of his career.

*Right: An exhibition match at Warwick Golf Club in 1901.
Vardon (in striped jacket, sitting) defeated amateur champion Harold
Hilton (standing third from left) on the final hole .*

A short time after the exhibition match, Vardon came to the final hole of the Open Championship needing a five to tie with Taylor. Playing short of the green in two, he managed to get it. The 36-hole play-off was arranged for the following Monday. Already unsettled by their earlier match together, Taylor lost by four shots. It was Vardon's first Open Championship title and the beginning of what was to prove a glorious career.

The following year at Hoylake, the title went to the Amateur Champion, Harold Hilton. Vardon regained it in 1898 and again in 1899. He also finished runner-up in 1900, 1901 and 1902 in an amazing run of form lasting six years which had taken him from a virtual unknown to becoming the dominant player of the age. At Prestwick in 1903 Vardon won again, pushing his brother Tom into second place. He was now openly acknowledged as the greatest player in the world and was in great demand for exhibition matches and public appearances. But even while he was enjoying the acclaim, Harry Vardon was suffering from increasing bouts of ill-health. Kept secret from everyone except his closest friends, Vardon had fallen victim to tuberculosis and was secretly admitted to Mundesley Sanitorium in Norfolk later that year. Most probably, the TB had been contracted during an exhausting Exhibition Tour to the United States earlier in 1900.

In March 1900, the A. G. Spalding Company had manufactured their first rubber-core ball and named it the 'Vardon Flyer'. After agreeing the first sponsorship deal in golfing history, Vardon was

Right: *James Braid in mid-swing.*

brought out to promote it. Except for a quick trip home for the British Open at St Andrews, he spent most of the year playing exhibitions and touring the US. Despite beating Taylor in the US Open at Chicago, the trip was an exhausting experience.

Vardon, who had completed the whole tour, came back to England a sick man, but even after entering Mundesley Sanitorium, Vardon refused to let it affect his golf career. In between regular trips to Norfolk, he still competed in every Open Championship for the next five years finishing third, ninth, third, seventh and fifth – an amazing record considering his poor state of health and his putting. Struggling to hole anything inside three feet, Vardon's putting was becoming increasingly more erratic. By the 1910 Open at St Andrews, he had gone without a win for over seven years and was convinced his winning days were over. Then, in 1911, Harry Vardon's health began to improve, and so too surprisingly did his skill on the greens.

Entering the Open Championship at Sandwich in Kent in 1911, Vardon found that all his old form had returned. In what must have been a nostalgic comeback, Vardon beat Frenchman Arnaud Massey into second place to record his fifth Championship victory. Two years later he was back in the United States with Ted Ray, pursuing the same relentless exhibition tour that had ruined his health thirteen years before.

In 1914, Vardon finally moved ahead of Taylor and Braid to record his sixth Open win. Then came the war and golf was suspended for six years, by which time Harry Vardon was 50 years old. With his best days behind him, he still managed to tie fourteenth place in the 1920 Open championship at Deal, as well as finishing runner-up to Ted Ray in the US Open at Inverness. A short time later his glorious career was finished, and he spent his final years as club professional at South Herts Golf Club at Totteridge. Perhaps his golfing life was best summed up by his friend and rival J. H. Taylor: 'There was a gentleness inherent in Vardon's conduct that reminded one of his easy persuasiveness when hitting the ball. Kindly and considerate and without harshness, he looked upon the world with tolerance and understanding, and went his way oblivious of the fact that in him was to be seen its greatest golfer.'

After years of English dominance, a new Scottish hero called James Braid emerged to win the 1901 Open Championship at Muirfield. Standing 6 feet 2 inches, he was a tall, gangling man with a whiplash swing that featured a pronounced knee dip at impact. At 30 years of age, he appeared at first sight an unlikely hero for Scottish golf but James Braid went on to dominate the Open Championship for nine years from 1901 to 1910. His amazing record of winning five times, being runner-up three times and two other top-ten finishes was unrivalled in his, or any other era.

Braid was born on 6 February 1870, in Earlsferry, a small town fifteen miles south of St Andrews. Unusually for that part of Scotland, his father did not play golf and was entirely against his son playing it. At thirteen, James Braid was forced to take up an apprenticeship as a carpenter/joiner in a village over three miles away. A six-mile walk each day ensured that Braid had very little time for golf practice. Therefore, it was a testament to his skill and dedication that he was a scratch golfer by his sixteenth birthday.

At nineteen he left home to work at St Andrews. Striking up a friendship with Andrew Kirkaldy and Alex Herd, he was often seen playing the Old Course with one or both of them. It proved to be a good education for the Scot, because two years later he won the prestigious and aptly named Braid Hills tournament in Edinburgh. Then in 1893 he left Scotland and took up a post as an apprentice club-maker at the Army and Navy Store in London. With the freedom to play on Sundays (in Scotland the playing of golf on the Sabbath was still banned), Braid's golf game also profited by the presence of his cousin, Douglas Rolland, at nearby Limpsfield Golf Club.

In 1894, James Braid turned professional and played his first exhibition match with Rolland at Limpsfield. He also played his first Open Championship at Sandwich the same year where he tied for a creditable tenth place, fifteen strokes behind the eventual winner, J. H. Taylor. After missing the following Championship at St Andrews, Braid had his first taste of playing Taylor in an exhibition match at West Drayton. Braid later wrote about their halved game 'that he remembered nothing more vividly in all his golfing life than this match'. His good showing against the two-times Open Champion led to more exhibition matches, as well

as the post of club professional at Romford in Essex.

The early years at Romford were a time of transition for Braid. He was well known for his long driving, but was also known for his erratic putting method – at Hoylake in 1897 he should have won comfortably, but lost out on the final green to Harold Hilton after persistently three-putting his way through the championship. He did the same again at St Andrews in 1900, and soon his career was in danger of ending before it had really begun.

James Braid's putting problems were twofold. First, his overall vision was poor after he had had lime thrown into his eyes whilst training as a joiner's apprentice. Secondly, like many of his fellow professionals, he putted out with a driving cleek (the equivalent of a modern 3-iron). A common enough method with greens much rougher than today's, it involved crouching over the putt and 'popping' the ball forward. Obviously unsuited to such a maneuver the tall gangling Braid searched desperately for another solution. It came early in 1901, when Braid was persuaded by club-maker William Mills to try out his new range of aluminum-headed putters. After many hours of practice, his first professional outing with the new putter was the Open Championship at Muirfield. It proved to be a tremendous turning point.

Despite driving out-of-bounds with his opening tee-shot at the 1901 event, and finishing with a disastrous round of 80, Braid recov-

Below: *A large gallery watches Braid drive-off during an exhibition match at Newquay in 1903.*

ered well in the remaining three rounds. His score of 309 was enough to beat Harry Vardon into second place by three strokes, and Taylor into third by four. James Braid's momentous victory at Muirfield had finally given the golfing world the 'Great Triumvirate'.

In 1902, the British Open at Hoylake was won by another Scot, Alex Herd. A small built, undemonstrative character, he was never as popular with the golfing public as the other three professionals. Despite this, Herd was to prove the ideal partner for Braid in many exhibition matches against the English pair of Vardon and Taylor.

With national pride at stake, these England/Scotland matches became increasingly popular with the golfing public. In 1905, Braid won the Open at St Andrews by five clear shots from J. H. Taylor. It was his second title in five years, and the Scottish newspapers shouted loudly about the 'English' challenge of Vardon and Taylor being put to flight.

With public interest almost at fever pitch, an international challenge match was quickly arranged between the four professionals. Backed by Lord Riddell for England and Sir Edward Hulton for Scotland, the 'Great Foursome' was to be played over St Andrews, Troon, Lytham St Annes and Deal. With the prize money standing at £400 a side, the opening match was arranged at St Andrews – two months after the Open had been held there.

With almost twelve thousand people turning up to watch, the atmosphere was strongly partisan in favor of the Scottish pair. With loud cheers every time an English putt was missed, the normally calm Vardon threatened to quit. Persuaded to carry on by his partner Taylor, the English pair finished two holes down. At Troon, Vardon and Taylor gained their revenge by performing brilliantly to win the day fourteen holes up.

Despite Braid and Herd pulling the deficit back to only seven holes at Lytham, and Vardon's attack of tuberculosis the night before the final leg at Deal, the match at Troon had effectively killed off the Scottish challenge.

Despite losing the 'Great Foursome' match, Braid was at his golfing peak and went on to record his third Open win at Muirfield in 1906. His victory at Prestwick two years later in 1908 made it four championships, with St Andrews in 1910 totaling his triumphs to five. It was a remarkable effort for someone who had only turned professional ten years before. Five Open Championship titles in nine years had made James Braid the most successful golfer of all time.

In the Open Championship of 1913, James Braid's eyes were so bad that he played the whole week at Hoylake in dark glasses. The newspapers and golf magazines reporting from that championship talked about Braid's career as if it was over – which effectively it was.

Braid spent his final years teaching at the Walton Heath in Surrey. Even up to his death in 1950, aged 80, his love of the game was undiminished. He played every day, weather permitting, regularly beating players half his age on many occasions. James Braid remained a quiet, undemonstrative man throughout his life. Like the other two members of the 'Great Triumvirate', his contribution to golf was considerable, with J. H. Taylor, he helped form the first Professional Golfers Association, as well as designing innumerable golf courses across Britain. Unlike Vardon and Taylor, a fear of sea crossings meant that he never ventured across to America to challenge for the American title. Motion sickness was also the reason he never owned a motor car and he resisted owning a telephone because

In 1860 at St Andrews a small group of women were found playing golf on waste ground near the town railway station. Led by Mrs Robert Boothby, the wife of a scratch member of the R&A, they had secretly taken advantage of a few rough holes marked out by caddies who used it in their spare time. It was essentially a private pleasure that was to have very public consequences; soon after they began, the shocking sight of women hitting golf balls, even on waste ground, brought a tidal wave of male condemnation and ridicule. The women were publicly rebuked and ordered to turn in their golf clubs.

Golf in nineteenth-century Scotland was not considered a suitable pastime for the wives of gentleman. Apart from the common male prejudices of a woman's place being in the home, the main objection focused on the actual muscular effort involved in striking the ball. At a time when physical exertion was considered a preoccupation of the lower orders, the idea of a woman raising a golf club above her head absolutely horrified most men. In 1890, Lord Wellwood spoke on behalf of many men when he wrote: 'The postures and gestures requisite for a full swing are not particularly graceful when the player is clad in female dress.'

Despite most women golfers being limited to a discreet putt or occasional chip when no one was looking, the general opinion was that even this was too much. Earlier in 1867, *Cornhill Magazine* reported the particularly irate opinion of one military man who found his foursomes opponent accompanied by his wife and sister-in-law. He commented, 'The links are not the place for women, they talk incessantly, never stand still, and if they do the wind won't allow their dresses to stand still.'

The unsuitability of women to golf was obviously a long-held view in Scotland. As early as 1565, Mary, Queen of Scots, was openly accused at her trial of unseemly behavior for 'playing golf in the fields by Seton' only days after the death of her

Right: *Competitors at the first 'international' golf meeting at Ranelagh in 1894.*

Top left: *Playing golf in ankle-length skirts and starched collars.*

Above: *A social frame of golf at Newquay in 1903.*

husband, Lord Darnley. Yet before the end of the nineteenth century, a remarkable revolution had taken place; most of the male prejudices which had restricted women's early golf had been swept away, and by 1890 women golfers could be found playing on almost every golf course in Scotland. Three years later they had formed the Ladies Golf Union, bringing with it a framework by which women's tournaments were officially sanctioned. Also in 1893, the first British Ladies' Championship had been held at Lytham St Annes.

So what triggered this amazing turnaround? Like most things that happened during the latter years of the nineteenth century, it was part of a much wider social evolution. In the

early years, however, it was Mrs Boothby and her golfing friends who made the initial breakthrough. After the debacle near St Andrews, a sympathetic member of the Royal and Ancient, David Burie, had promised to look out for a less 'public' place where the ladies could play golf. Seven years later, he found a spot on the seaward side of the Royal and Ancient Clubhouse.

Little more than a putting green, it was just the start that the determined Mrs Boothby was looking for. She quickly formed the first St Andrews Ladies Golf Club, with herself as President and David Burie as secretary, and levied a small subscription to provide for someone to cut the grass and tend the holes. All male mutterings about it being the end of civilization were ignored, and on 5 September 1867 the first ladies' course was officially opened.

However, the war was not completely won; soon after the putting course opened, a man arrived with orders from the landowner, Captain Cheape, to eject forcibly the women from the green unless they agreed to pay rent. The matter was taken up by David Burie who negotiated an annual rent of £7. Cheape agreed and soon the ladies' putting course became a 'very charming feature' of St Andrews golfing life.

Things were slowly beginning to change for women golfers. In his book *The Royal and Ancient Game*, published in 1875, Robert Clark wrote: 'The skills of the fair competitors is by no means to be despised, and on their own ground, the best of them would be backed freely against the cracks of the R. and A ...'

This growing respect for ladies' golf was indicative of the changes to come. There was still no question of women being allowed on the Old Course to play but, following the example of the ladies of St Andrews, other women's golf clubs were formed with varying degrees of success.

The oldest ladies' golf club in England was formed at Royal North Devon in 1868. Laid out on spare ground near Pebble Ridge, it was called The Westward Ho and North Devon Ladies Club. Despite being over five hundred miles from St Andrews, the female members experienced the same sort of difficulties with male golfers as their Scottish counterparts. Run by the men's committee, it was ruled that the course could only be used every other Saturday from May to October, and under no circumstances must any other club 'besides a wooden putter' be used on the links. Not surprisingly, the ladies' club disbanded in 1878, only to reform later in 1890. During these vital twelve years a huge change in social attitude enabled women golfers to play on the same course as the men.

The first British Ladies' Championship was held at Lytham St Annes in 1893. The tournament, won by the youthful Lady Margaret Scott, proved to be a major turning point for British women's golf. During the early 1900s, when Victorian hypocrisy was at its height, every social or sporting occasion

Above: *A 1910 advertisement for Helsby golf balls.*

was considered solely in terms of it's being fashionable or not. After Lady Margaret Scott's victory at Lytham the glittering social world of London society made her something of a celebrity. The daughter of Lord Eldon, she had the advantage of learning to play on her father's private golf course in the family grounds. In a feature in *Golf Illustrated* magazine, her swing was described as 'graceful yet powerful'. Attractive and personable, Lady Margaret Scott personified the game of golf for many and contributed to its increasing popularity amongst women.

Right: *Lady Margaret Scott, winner of the first British Ladies Championship in 1893.*

Following on from the first Ladies' Championship, the Ladies' Golf Union cleverly orchestrated an open golf meeting at the highly fashionable Ranelagh Club in London. A short nine-hole course had been quickly laid out in the park amidst the conifers and ornamental ponds, over which teams contested for various prizes including the grandiose title of 'International Ladies Champion'. With the cream of London society rolling up in their open carriages just to watch, it proved a great advertisement for the game and it soon established itself as an important event on the social calendar.

The golf days at Ranelagh also effected another desirable bonus. When the Ladies Golf Union was formed in 1893, fewer than twenty clubs were involved. Many of these were little more than extended par-three courses with an old greenkeeper's shed acting as clubhouse, but after the highly public success of Ranelagh things started to change. At Formby in 1896, a group of influential women golfers banded together to buy their own clubhouse at a cost of £300. The course itself was leased from the main club, but its affairs were (and still are) run entirely independently from the men. In the later years of the nineteenth century, even those women's golf clubs without facilities were increasingly offered rooms of their own inside the main clubhouse, as well as restricted access to the main course.

Despite the ladies' nine-hole course at Littlestone being openly described as the 'hen-run,' women golfers started to establish themselves in this hitherto male-dominated world, extra concessions were asked for and given: for example, the golf course was to be set aside on one day per week exclusively for the use of women members. That achieved, the women demanded the right to play on the previously sacrosanct men-only weekend. Despite only a grudging agreement from most of the men, the women finally got their way. As the nineteenth century came to a close, women golfers had succeeded in getting their foot in the clubhouse door. Their rapid progress within half a century, from playing on waste ground near St Andrews railway station to having golf courses of their own, was nothing less than remarkable.

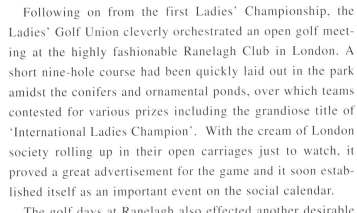

Left: *The present-day ladies clubhouse at Formby Golf Club.*

Left: *British Prime Minister David Lloyd George.*

In 1910, an unusual 72-hole challenge match was arranged over Walton Heath and Sunningdale between top female golfer Cecil Leitch and the great amateur champion, Harold Hilton. Watched by thousands of interested onlookers, it was arranged so that both players would drive from the men's tees, but Leitch was compensated for her lack of strength by receiving a handicap allowance of one stroke every second hole. After four rounds in front of a large, mainly female gallery, Cecil Leitch eventually triumphed two and one. Striking a blow for British women's golf, the significance of the result was certainly not lost on the men watching.

The match itself received a great deal of publicity. Played during a time when women's issues were at the forefront of the political agenda, Cecil Leitch's win in this battle of the sexes was hailed as a triumph for women everywhere. Not surprisingly, the game of golf was seen by the Women's Movement in the early 1900s as a stronghold of male privilege and prejudice. In retaliation, golf greens all over the Home Counties were destroyed by suffragettes and even the Liberal Prime Minister, David Lloyd George, had been debagged while playing golf at Walton Heath. Questions were asked in the House of Commons by angry golfing politicians, demanding an end to such behavior, but the women's leader, Emily Pankhurst, was determined to continue the fight. In February 1913, *The Suffragette* magazine commented: 'Some people say the suffragettes having acted very unwisely in destroying golf greens because this has made golfers very angry, yet what is there to fear from their anger? What have (male) golfers ever done for the Suffragette Cause, and what will they ever do if they are left in peace to play their game?'

Around the turn of the century, the greatest battle most women golfers had to face was playing golf in the fashionable dress of the period. Usually consisting of a blouse with stiff-starched collar, tie, military hacking jacket and tweed ankle-length skirt, it proved to be an enormous disadvantage and restricted most women on the putting green. Changes to more practical clothing, like the woman's right to vote, did eventually come; but for the first two decades of the British Ladies Championship, buttoned and restrictive golfing attire was still the order of the day.

After winning the first three titles in succession from 1893 onwards, Lady Margaret Scott had announced her retirement from competitive golf. She was followed in The Ladies' Championship by a string of fine women golfers including May Hezlet, the youngest of three talented Irish sisters. Winning her first title in 1899 aged only 17, she went on to equal Lady Margaret Scott's record of three Ladies' Championships with further wins in 1902 and 1907. Another great champion of the pre-war period was Wimbledon Ladies' Singles winner, Lottie Dodd. Having dominated the women's singles since 1887, she became bored with tennis and turned to golf for a new challenge. A charismatic personality who brought a great deal of interest to women's golf, she won her one and only British Ladies title in 1904.

The first great champion of the women's game was Dorothy Campbell from North Berwick. She had followed her British Ladies' victory at Birkdale in 1909 by winning the United States Ladies' Championship at Merion the same year. The first woman golfer to achieve this remarkable and unique British/American double, she almost made it a 'triple' the following year when she won the American and Canadian titles, only to be defeated by Miss G. Suttie in the British Championships.

The United States Ladies' event had been inaugurated two years after the first

Left: *Cecil Leitch in action at Sunningdale in 1910.*

Right: *Ladies golf and tennis champion Lottie Dodd.*

British Ladies' Championship in 1895. Played at Meadowbrook Golf Club in New York, the first winner was Mrs Charles Brown, with a score of 132. Established the same year as the men's first US Amateur and US Open titles, it was also the only time that stroke-play was used to decide the winner. The following year, in 1896, the American Ladies' Championship changed to match play and has remained that way ever since. In the early years of the championship and prior to Dorothy Campbell's historic win, the dominant American woman golfer was Beatrix Hoyt from Shinnecock Hills. She had won her first title in 1896 as a sixteen year old schoolgirl, and then went on to notch up two more consecutive Championships before her nineteenth birthday.

The early 1900s, saw the emergence of a more dedicated type of American woman golfer. Starting at the Midlothian Golf Club in 1907, the event came to be dominated by two sisters – Harriot and Margaret Curtis. Having played golf from an early age, they were both dedicated to the game and went on to win the US title once and three times respectively. Later they became the driving force behind the first Curtis Cup international matches between America and Britain in the early 1930s. According to Harriot Curtis, the cup offered in their name was 'to stimulate friendly rivalry between the women golfers of many lands'. An admirable sentiment, this has seen the Curtis Cup matches become an integral part of the women's game.

The entry for the Ladies' Championship had soared to over one hundred applicants by the time Alexa Stirling won her first Championship in 1916. Known for her superb iron play, she had spent her formative golfing years with her childhood friend, Bobby Jones. Aged nineteen, she won her first title at Belmont Springs in Boston, then had to wait out the war years before making it three consecutive Championship wins in 1919 and 1920.

Apart from Alexa Stirling, a sixteen-year-old from Rhode Island, Glenna Collett, had also impressed everyone in the 1919 Championship at Shawnee Country Club. Accurate and deceptively powerful, she was destined to become the 'Bobby Jones' of American women's golf, winning six championships, three of them in a row, eight times a finalist and six times a low qualifying medalist. Glenna Collett won her first Ladies' Championship in 1922 at Greenbrier, West Virginia, and again in 1925, 1928, 1929, 1930 and 1935. Later to become Glenna Collett-Vare, after marriage to Philadelphia businessman, Edwin Vare, she was the greatest American woman golfer of her era. After her third Ladies' title at Virginia Hot Springs in 1928, she was still in her mid-twenties, and considered almost unbeatable. Collett herself was looking for a new challenge and in 1929 she set her sights on the British Ladies' Championship at St Andrews. Unknown to her at the time, the greatest woman golfer in the history of the game was coming out of retirement to meet her – the legendary Joyce Wethered.

*Left: Originators of the Curtis Cup matches between Great Britain and the United States – Harriet and Margaret Curtis.*

No woman in the history of golf has come closer to mythical status than Joyce Wethered. Stories detailing her skill and powers of concentration are legendary, with Bobby Jones himself describing her in 1930 as 'The finest golfer I have ever seen'. He went on to say, .,. I have never played golf with anyone, man or woman, amateur or professional, who made me feel so utterly outclassed.'

A year later, Robert Harris, the 1925 Amateur Champion, was equally impressed. Describing a score of 72 Joyce Wethered had made around Royal North Devon, he said: 'It was the best round of golf I'd ever seen played. She had beaten the better ball of two ex-champions and a scratch player. There were no fireworks produced only faultless golf. Vardon, Duncan and Bobby Jones, when I played them, were wont to produce fireworks from time to time … but this round of Miss Wethered's was above that class.'

Born in 1901, Joyce played in her first competition when she was eighteen – reaching the semi-finals of the Surrey Ladies. A year later in 1920, she entered the qualifying rounds for the English Ladies' Championship at Sheringham. If making the final was a surprise, winning it was to prove an even greater one. Playing one of the legendary figures of the women's game, Cecil Leitch, Joyce found herself six down after the opening two holes of the afternoon round. With very little to lose, she started to assert her own game, and after clawing her way back, she eventually triumphed two and one, pulling off in her own words, 'The biggest surprise that ladies golf has ever had sprung upon it.'

The first of many memorable battles between the two women, Cecil Leitch later referred to one incident from that final which has since gone down in golf history. Talking about Wethered's amazing powers of concentration, she wrote: 'A train went rattling by, but so unconscious was she [Joyce] of her immediate surroundings, that she afterwards admitted she never as much heard it pass.' This ability to focus purely on her own game was perhaps Joyce Wethered's greatest asset.

After losing her British title to Cecil Leitch at Turnberry in 1921, Joyce got her revenge at Deal one year later, crushing her rival nine and seven in the final – a result which remains the greatest winning margin to this day. Still only 23, Joyce was entering her prime. The tall, gangling youth of four years before was now an assured and experienced competitor. By 1925, she would have entered five English Championships and won them all.

Away from the drama of competition, she was by nature a shy person. She took little part in the social whirl which attended such events and always preferred to practice alone. Despite this seemingly cold attitude, Joyce was universally well liked by her fellow competitors, as well as the large galleries which flocked to see her play. But by 1925, the strain of repeating such perfection was beginning to tell. Glenna Collett herself, described Wethered's problem some years later: 'To the onlooker she is phlegmatic, cold, no nerves. Yet after a strenuous week of Championship golf, she is forced to rest and leave golf for a fortnight or more.'

As with Bobby Jones, the pressure of competition took its toll. Always sick with nerves before an important match, Wethered was beginning to feel the strain of performing to such high standards. In a rare moment of insight, Joyce wrote in 1933: 'I know the feeling of standing on a tee with real fear in my heart, the match slipping away and the club feeling strange

Below left: *Churchman's cigarettes' caricature of Joyce Wethered.*

Below right: *An aspiring Victorian actress in golfing pose.*

and useless in my hands.' After winning her fifth straight English title in 1925, she decided never to play in the event again. By the time she entered the 1925 British Championship at Troon her mind was already set on retiring.

Matched against her in the final was old adversary Cecil Leitch. For Wethered the match was a very tense affair. Squandering a lead of two up with three to play, she eventually scrambled a win at the 37th. It had been the most difficult game of her career and shortly after, an exhausted Joyce Wethered publicly announced her retirement – aged just twenty-six.

The next four years were spent catching up on the life she had missed. During her absence, other British players came to the fore; Cecil Leitch had won her fourth Ladies' title in 1926 and regained her position as top woman golfer. Younger players were also coming on the scene like Enid Wilson and another future Ladies' Champion, Diana Fishwick.

By the Ladies' Championship of 1929, the golfing world had moved on. The balance of power had shifted from Britain to America, and with Wethered gone, it was American Glenna Collett who was setting the standards in women's golf. Then it was announced in the British newspapers that Glenna Collett would be challenging for the Ladies' Championship at St Andrews. For Joyce Wethered, the temptation to make a comeback proved too strong; the heady mixture of playing at her beloved St Andrews and the growing challenge of Glenna Collett was too much to resist.

Any doubts that she may have lost her competitive edge were quickly dispelled. Bernard Darwin of The *Times* described her progress to the final as a 'triumphal procession'. At the same time, in the other half of the draw, Glenna Collett was playing equally well. With both of them making the final, the stage was set for a classic match with the whole of St Andrews turning out to watch. Playing in front of five thousand people, Wethered found herself five down after nine

Above: *Great golfing rivals: Cecil Leitch and Joyce Wethered.*

holes. Then, in what seemed a replay of her 1920 Final, she pulled herself back into the game, eventually beating the tough American three and one. Afterwards, with two policeman clearing a path through the cheering crowds, Wethered reflected on the 'very trying experience' playing the final had been. Perhaps feeling she had nothing left to prove, she retired from competitive golf for the second time this time aged 30. By 1932, the pressure for her to return was growing. She was persuaded to play in the first Curtis Cup match at Wentworth, where she beat Glenna Collett six and four in the top singles.

In 1934 Joyce went to work in the golf department at Fortnum and Masons in London. Shortly after, the Ladies' Golf Union took away her amateur status, declaring that by trading on her reputation as a famous golfer, she had become a professional. Understandably, Joyce was upset and confused. Shortly afterwards, American millionaire Alex Finlay of Wanamakers offered her a reputed $30,000 to complete an exhibition tour of the United States. A huge sum at the time, Joyce reluctantly accepted and sailed off for the United States.

Depression-hit America welcomed her with open arms. Touring from coast to coast, her exhibition matches were always well attended. Bringing a touch of class to the proceedings, she played against all the top names of US golf – including Bobby Jones, Gene Sarazen, Walter Hagen, and not surprisingly, Glenna Collett.

Once back in England, Joyce Wethered continued to play the occasional exhibition match, but sadly it was not until 1947 that the LGU would reinstate her amateur status. In 1937, she married Sir John Heathcoat-Amory and took the title of Lady Heathcoat-Amory. In 1975 she was inducted into the Golf Hall of Fame at Pinehurst, North Carolina. The greatest woman golfer of all time, she now lives quietly in retirement in Devon, England.

In the early nineteenth century, golfers were labeled purely in terms of social class. A 'professional' was deemed to be anyone who made his living from the game, like caddies, ball-makers, club-makers and greenkeepers. As for the gentlemen golfers who regularly supplemented their living by playing for large wagers, they were looked on respectfully as 'sportsmen' and nothing more. While today such behavior would inevitably lead to the loss of amateur status, back then it was considered acceptable for a gentleman to back up his golfing skill with wagers and bets. With class differences far more marked than today, there was little need for the fine social distinctions of amateurs and professional. Both groups knew their place and these descriptions were hardly ever used.

The term 'amateur' was first thought to have been used after the inaugural Open Championship on 1860. Prestwick, looking to build on the success of the first event, announced the competition 'open to all the world' from the following year. Most people took this to mean amateurs were welcome as well. Certainly it did, but the word 'amateur' was never used and it was never intended to include anyone other than the 'sporting gentleman'. Indeed, Major Fairlie, who had first proposed the tournament, had wanted it restricted exclusively to gentleman golfers rather than the eight professionals who did eventually play.

By 1885, most clubs had regular scratch competitions to find their own champion. These were fairly local affairs, but often the fame of one particular player would spread beyond his own club. It heralded a new age of fine amateur golfers who, hardened by regular competition, were willing to take on the professionals at their own game. One such amateur was John Ball Jnr. Born in Liverpool, he shares the distinction – along with Bobby Jones and Harold Hilton – of being the only amateur golfer to win the Open Championship.

John Ball spent his early years caddying on the Royal Liverpool course. Highly regarded from a young age, he had competed in the Open for the first time in 1876, aged only fifteen and had finished in sixth place. In 1885, inspired by the prowess of their star member, the Royal Liverpool Club arranged an open amateur knock-out tournament. The first national event of its kind, it proved so successful that it led to the institution of the first Amateur Championship the following year. Perhaps more significantly, it led to the first official definition of an amateur golfer.

One of the entrants for the amateur knock-out tournament was Douglas Rolland, a stone-mason from Elie in Fife. Famed for his long driving, Rolland had already beaten John Ball in a previous challenge match. He had also been joint runner-up in

Below: *Teeing off at Aberdovey Golf Club in 1898.*

Above: *John Ball receiving congratulations after beating C. Aylmer 10 and 9 in the final of the 1910 British Amateur Championship at Hoylake.*

the previous Open Championship at Prestwick and had shared second and third place prize money with professional Willie Fernie. Sadly for Rolland, this was taken into account when he submitted his entry for the Hoylake event. It was decided that by accepting prize money in a professional tournament, he had deemed himself to be a non-amateur and was disqualified from

entering. In a situation that smacked of double standards, the Royal Liverpool Golf Club committee made little reference to the ten shillings prize money John Ball had received in 1876.

Despite having defined an 'amateur' as someone who did not accept prize money in competitions with professionals, Royal Liverpool's ruling only applied to their own tournament

Above: *Golfers and caddies at the turn of the century.*

Right: *John Ball had the best record of any British amateur. He won the Amateur Championship eight times and was one of only two British amateurs to win the Open Championship. The first time was in 1890; he was the first Englishman to do so.*

and was not binding on any other private club. However, for the proposed Amateur Championship one year later in 1886 it was decided that a much clearer definition was needed. After due consideration, the Royal Liverpool Golf Club ruled that an amateur should be:

'a golfer who has never made for sale any golf clubs, balls, or any articles connected with the game, who had never carried clubs for hire after attaining the age of fifteen years, and who has not carried clubs for hire at any time within six years of the date on which the competition begins each year; who has never received any consideration for playing in a match or for giving lessons in the game, and who, for a period of five years prior to the 1st of September, 1886, has never received a money prize in an open (championship) competition.'

This was an historic definition which forms the basis on which amateur golfers are judged even today. It is also significant in that it still continued to label caddies under the title of professional. It is not known how many golfers were disquali-

Left: *Amateur champion Harold H. Hilton, immortalized by Sir Leslie Ward, alias 'Spy'.*

fied from entering by this new rule, but the first Amateur Championship got under way and was won by local man, Allan MacFie. Curiously, for many years the competition at Hoylake was not recognized as the first Amateur Championship – that honor belonged to the 1886 event at St Andrews. It was finally reinstated by the Royal and Ancient in 1922, after they assumed sole responsibility for organizing the championship.

The early years of the Amateur Championship were dominated by the man who had effectively inspired its inception. John Ball won the title a record eight times, from 1888 to 1912 (a record that takes into account his three year absence in the Boer War). The crowning achievement of his career came with winning the Professional Open Championship of 1890 at Prestwick. By becoming the first Englishman to win the title, he broke the Scottish stranglehold on the tournament that stretched back to Willie Park in 1860.

A small man with quick hands, Ball was a natural swinger of the club. He lived his life as he played golf – simply and without fuss. Building on the success he laid down, the period from 1890 to 1900 can be described as the amateur players' golden age. Two years after Ball had won at Prestwick, Harold Hilton won the first of his two Open titles at Muirfield, with his second triumph coming in 1897 at his home course of Hoylake. Great rivals throughout most of their careers, the similarities between the two men were striking. Both had been born in Liverpool and worked their way up as caddies at Royal Liverpool. While Hilton was more than ten years younger than John Ball, he had followed closely in his illustrious rival's footsteps. A small man of powerful physique, his quick, flashing golf swing often resulted in his cap falling to the ground at impact.

Despite playing at the peak of John Ball's career, Hilton still managed to win four Amateur titles, one US Amateur Competition in 1911, and a second Open Championship at Hoylake in 1897.

With the suspension of the Amateur and Open Championships from 1915 to 1919, Harold Hilton retired from golf to become editor of *Golf Monthly* magazine. His career, which had brought rich rewards in terms of championship titles, had paved the way for other amateurs to follow. When competitive golf finally resumed after World War I, a new generation of amateurs had pushed to the foreground. The old guard of Ball, Hilton, J. E. Laidlay, F. G. Tait and Jock Hutchinson, had all been replaced by the new challengers who would dominate the amateur game well into the 1920s – players like Tolley, Holderness and Roger Wethered, runner-up in the 1921 Open to Jock Hutchinson.

In Amateur and Open Championships, these men would carry the mantle of British golf at home and abroad. But with the increasing might of the Americans in the late 1920s, led primarily by Bobby Jones, British golf began to slip quietly into the position of the underdog. Until the outbreak of World War II, British golf was not only losing its top amateur titles to the United States but was losing its professional championships as well. The balance of power had shifted and it was American rather than British amateurs who dominated golf.

Left: *A painting of Harold Hilton by J. J. Inglis.*

**1** Silver confectionery dish suported by golf clubs, 1910.    **2** Rolling or Cylinder head putter, 1905.    **3** Triumph putter, 1920.    **4** Severe swan-neck putter, 1920.    **5** OKE patent long-nosed putter, 1925.
**6** Rib-faced iron, 1900.    **7** Patent driver, 1900.    **8** Brown's patent rake iron, 1900.    **9** Child's cup and saucer, Austrian, 1905.
**10** Colonel patent paper tee with Bramble golf ball, 1908.
**11** Royal Doulton jug decorated with early 17th century golfing figures, 1913.    **12** Captain's medal with tartan ribbon, Heather Golf Club (no longer in existence), 1810.    **13** Paperweight, golfer figure in tweed clothing, 1900.

Late in 1887, Robert Lockhart wandered into Old Tom Morris's shop in St Andrews and bought six hickory clubs and two dozen guttie balls. After explaining they were for his friend in America, Lockhart asked for the equipment to be forwarded to his address in New York. For Tom Morris and his staff it was not a particularly unusual request. Accustomed to sending golfing implements to all corners of the British Empire, Morris bundled the clubs up and sent them off shortly afterwards. No doubt pleased to have fulfilled his obligation, Robert Lockhart had little idea of the historic chain of events he had just set into motion.

The golf clubs and guttie balls which had been ordered on behalf of his fellow Scottish exile John G. Reid finally arrived in the middle of winter, but even with temperatures around the Hudson River near freezing point, Lockhart could not resist the temptation to try them out. Though completely unaware of his actions, he was possibly the first person to play golf in America for almost one hundred years.

On 22 February 1888 – George Washington's birthday – the weather broke fine and clear and Reid was again unable to suppress his enthusiasm. Gathering together a bemused group of six friends, he marched down to a Yonkers cow pasture and marked out three short holes. Since there were not enough clubs to go around, Reid squared off against John Upham, while the others formed the gallery.

Shortly after, New York was paralyzed by one of the severest blizzards of all time. Golf was suspended over winter and the opportunity was taken to order more clubs from Scotland. With the consignment taking months to arrive, the friends took turns using John Reid's original six clubs and guttie balls. Obviously bitten by the golfing bug, the group took over a larger plot of land located at North Broadway and Shonnard Place. Never bothering to buy the lease, or even pay rent, they laid out a rough course of six holes with circular greens measuring twelve feet in diameter.

The ordered clubs arrived during the summer and the golfing friends soon became a regular sight on the North Broadway 'links'. With the game of golf completely unknown in the United States, strolling New Yorkers would stop and stare in amazement at the antics of these golfing friends. Then almost nine months after they began playing, John Reid proposed that their golfing society should be given the official title of the St Andrews Golf Club of Yonkers. Named after the place the clubs were bought, the first golf club in the United States was officially formed on 14 November 1888.

Later forced to give up their six-hole course at North Broadway, the St Andrews Club moved to a 34-acre site a short distance away. It was an old apple orchard, therefore it was only a matter of time before the group of golfing friends were labeled as the 'Apple Tree Gang'.

As their numbers grew, so did the need for a larger area to play on. Driven by an increasing number of younger members, the St Andrews Club established a nine-hole course at Gray Oaks. This was their last move before finally relocating to their present home at Mount Hope in 1897. Unlike before, there was room enough to build the first eighteen-hole layout

Left: *John Reid, the father of American golf.*

Above: *The clubhouse at Shinnecock Hills, site of the 1995 US Open. It was designed in the 1890's by leading architect Stanford White.*

in the United States. Setting a trend which the rest of American golf was to follow, St Andrews of Yonkers remains the oldest established golf club in the United States.

It was thought that golf had been played in America at least one hundred years before the advent of the 'Apple Tree Gang'. Reports in a 1786 Charleston newspaper mentioned the formation of an early golf club at Harleston Green. At the same time across the state border in Savannah another early golf course was described in a local newspaper, but how these links had come about and what actually happened to them has never been satisfactorily explained.

Unlike those early golf clubs at Harleston Green and Savannah, golf quickly became established in the latter years of the nineteenth century. From those first primitive beginnings on the Yonkers cow pasture, interest in the

game took off at an alarming rate. The second oldest club in the United States after St Andrews was founded at Middlesborough, Kentucky, by expatriate Englishmen in 1889. The land on which the nine-hole course was established was originally the site of an iron foundry. In contrast, the nine-hole course at Newport, Rhode Island, was an altogether more luxurious affair.

Formed in 1890 by a syndicate of millionaires including Cornelius Vanderbilt, sugar magnate Theodore Havermeyer and John Jacob Astor, it became the venue for the first United States Open in 1895.

Shinnecock Hills was formed one year after Rhode Island, in 1891. Situated on nearby Long Island, the course was designed by Scottish professional, Willie Dunn. Renowned in modern times as one of the finest golf courses in the world, the original twelve-hole links was built along the scenic Great Peconic Bay at Southampton. It was considered the first proper golf course in the United States.

In keeping with the luxurious 'country club' concept of early American golf, the Brookline Country Club in Boston, Massachusetts, was next to be formed in 1892. By 1893, golf had reached the Mid-west, when the country's first eighteen-hole course was laid out at Wheaton, Illinois. Home of the Chicago Golf Club, it was also the brainchild of Charles Blair MacDonald  one of the most influential and controversial figures in early American golf.

Above: *Horton Smith, winner of the first US Masters.*

Known for his abrasive outbursts, C B MacDonald cut his golfing teeth on the Old Course at St Andrews, where he was sent for schooling by his wealthy businessman father. Destined to become one of the leading legislators of the fledgling United States Golf Association, his early reputation was of someone who had an uncompromising attitude to the rules and traditions of golf.

Over the years, Charles MacDonald's black-and-white outlook on the game brought him many critics, especially as his behavior on the course did not often match his gentlemanly ideals off it, and it was a direct result of MacDonald's blustering, that there were calls for a national body which could legislate in disputes, establish rules, standardize play and organize future events. A meeting was called for 22 December 1894 and was attended by representatives of the five main clubs including St Andrews of Yonkers, Newport (Rhode Island), Shinnecock Hills, Chicago and Brookline Country Club. In the discussion that followed, sugar tycoon Theodore Havermeyer was elected over John Reid as the first President of the newly formed Amateur Golf Association of the United States. Later to become the United States Golf Association, plans were immediately made to stage two major tournaments – one amateur and one professional – for the following year at Newport Golf Club. Both competitions would be held during the same week, and would be known as the United States Amateur Championship and the United States Open Championship.

The early years of the championship were dominated by two men – Walter J Travis and Jerome D Travers. Despite their similar sounding names, both men were complete opposites. Travis was an Australian whose family moved to the United Stated when he was four. A brooding, dark-bearded man, he did not take up golf until he was 35. Naturally gifted, he went on to win three Amateur Championships in four years (1900–3) and one British title in 1904 at Sandwich.

By comparison, Jerome Travers came from a rich society family on Long Island. Playing golf by the age of nine, he won his first US Amateur at Euclid, Cleveland, aged only twenty.

Left: *Two American golfing greats – Francis Ouimet (left) and Bobby Jones.*

year's Amateur Championship at Beverly Country Club, Chicago, was won by Francis Ouimet.

After Ouimet came the transatlantic competitions of the 1930s. Following in Bobby Jones's footsteps, top American amateurs regularly traveled over to compete in the British Amateur. Certainly the most successful before he turned professional was W. Lawson Little Jnr. No doubt benefiting from Bobby Jones's absence, he won two US Amateur titles in 1934 and 1935 – at Brookline and Cleveland which he matched with a British double in the same years at Prestwick and Royal Lytham. Unlike those previous champions, both American and British, who suffered because of the war years, Lawson Little went on to forge a successful professional career, including his win in the US Open of 1940.

Lawson Little's transition from the amateur to professional game was smooth enough, but for others it was less so. Of the great champions who won the United States Amateur titles, only a small percentage actually turned professional after their win. Those who did, like Jerome Travers, quickly returned to their amateur roots. Others like Francis Ouimet, who had his amateur status removed for working for a sporting goods company, lobbied hard to have it returned. Bobby Jones, the ultimate amateur, stayed clear of the professional game all his life, despite very generous financial inducements to do otherwise. Amateur golf, it seemed, was in the American blood and turning professional for huge financial gain just was not tempting enough.

Like his great rival, Travers dominated the US Amateur, winning his four championships in 1907, 1908, 1912 and 1913.

Sadly for both players, the two-year break for World War I saw the end of both their careers. By the end of the war, Travis was too old to return competitively, while Travers developed intermittent problems with alcohol. Later, when the Depression struck America in the 1930s, it hit Jerome Travers hard and he turned professional. He had beaten the great Walter Hagen in 1917, but the years had taken their toll and he quickly gave up. Travers died in 1951 aged just 54.

After the war, Jerome Travers's mantle was taken up by possibly the best generation of American amateurs ever seen. Charles 'Chick' Evans won his second US Amateur at Engineers Country Club in 1920 to confirm his position as top amateur – this followed his 1916 pre-war double of United Stated Amateur and Open titles. He was quickly followed in the 1921–2 National Amateur by winners Jesse and Jess – Guilford and Sweetser. In 1923 at Flossmoor Country Club, Illinois, Max Marsden won his only title, and then came the era of Robert Tyre Jones Jnr. The greatest amateur golfer to ever live, he won the US Amateur in five of the next seven seasons from 1924 to 1930.

Throughout the 1920s, the standard of amateur golf in America was incredibly high. In 1926, the same year he won both the British and American Open crowns, Bobby Jones was beaten at Baltusrol in the US Amateur final by George Von Elm. After Jones's sudden retirement in 1930, the following

Right: *United States Open and Amateur Champion, Jerome Travers.*

'Golf may be played anywhere – that is, anywhere where there is room, but the quality of golf will depend upon the kind of place it is played on, and the manner which the ground is laid out and kept.'

This was the view expressed by writer Garden Smith on golf architecture in 1898. Outlining the basic principles involved in building a golf course, his views were probably considered quite radical in the latter part of the nineteenth century. Even allowing for the boom in golf course construction during the late Victorian Age, most traditionalists believed that nature was the only true architect with all man-made additions falling woefully short. But as wonderful as Mother Nature is, she has yet to find a way to prepare tightly mown greens, split fairway from rough and plant flagsticks; all that is done by a golf course architect.

Unfortunately, nothing is known about the very first golf course designers. Certainly Nature offered a helping hand, but it is more likely that early links like St Andrews, Leith and Bruntsfield all evolved form the first primitive target games

played by the local inhabitants. Then, as the game of golf took hold and became more popular, the first rudimentary targets were replaced over the centuries by longer, more defined golf holes.

Probably the earliest known and most prolific golf course architect was Tom Morris Snr. Considered one step up from a professional, his job description at Prestwick included the title 'Keeper of the Greens'. This meant that apart from his other duties, he was expected to act as greenkeeper and offer advice on any future course alterations. After his Open Championship successes of the early 1860s, Morris became the first golf professional actually to be commissioned to design other courses. Despite having Royal North Devon, Royal Dornoch and Lahinch in Ireland to his credit, some of his original designs were fairly simplistic compared with the great courses situated there today. However, to Old Tom's credit, his later designs did include some radical ideas which have since formed the basis of every golf course constructed today.

It was Morris who first developed the concept of designing golf courses with two separate loops of holes. Before then, it was traditional to follow the Scottish concept of nine holes out with nine holes back. An imaginative step, it avoided the boredom of playing an extended series of holes in the same direction, with the same wind conditions. It also offered the benefit of two starting points when the course became busy, and his later course at Royal County Down was based on this principle.

Following Tom Morris's example, other well-known golf professionals also turned to golf course design as a lucrative sideline. Among the first in the late 1870s was Morris's fellow Scot, Tom Dunn. He moved south to become professional/ greenkeeper at the London Scottish Golf Club in Wimbledon, where he helped enlarge the course from seven to eighteen holes. Joined by his brother Willie in 1878, he went on to design courses at Tooting Bec in 1888 and Bournemouth in

1894. Having established one of the first specialist golf course design companies at Merrick Park in Bournemouth, he proceeded to lay out over 137 golf courses world wide. Willie Dunn Jnr also went on to a successful career in course design, which included a prestigious commission from W. E. Vanderbilt for Shinnecock Hills.

Another respected golf course designer of the period was two-times Open Champion, Willie Park Jnr. The most innovative golf professional of the late nineteenth century, he concentrated on designing for the upper end of the market, with projects at West Hill, Huntercombe, as well as legendary Sunningdale. Park also foresaw the need for stricter guidelines in the types of courses being built. Golf courses had been springing up almost everywhere in the boom period of the 1890s, and many were little more than open fields with a tee at one end and a hole at the other. Park observed the futility of building such courses, observing that as the standard of golf became higher, so these poorly conceived courses would become quickly obsolete. He was eventually proved right, with prominent course designer Tom Simpson later describing the last years of the nineteenth century as the 'dark ages of golf architecture'.

Prior to amazing growth in the number of golf courses built from 1896 to 1910, few courses existed outside Scotland. With golf still considered primarily a 'Scottish' game, many of the courses built, especially the ones in England, had links-type features incorporated into them. These features were fine if the course was built on the coast, but looked distinctly out of place anywhere else. As such, most inland courses built during this period were usually substandard and boring to play on. With the clay-based land of southern England being totally unsuited to the links-type golf courses being built on it, many early golf courses met with universal condemnation. A Scottish golfer signing himself as 'Baffy' wrote to *Golf* magazine in 1895

Left: *Harry Colt was one of the new breed of golf course architects.*

commenting: 'Golf is attempted to be played in England on many places about as fitted for the game as a summer fallow is for the game of cricket ... We are all aware that one cannot make a silk purse out of a sow's ear, or a proper links out of an old park, or fields of good inland pasture.'

After 1900, golf course design became the domain of the talented amateurs who had cut their architectural teeth on the sand and heather courses of southern England. Emerging to challenge the part-time golf professional/course designer, this new breed had made golf course architecture their full-time profession. Of course, great British Open Champions like Vardon, Braid and J. H. Taylor were always in demand, but it was full-time designers like John Abercromby, Herbert Fowler, Harry Colt and, later, Sir Guy Campbell and Fred Hawtree, who were proving to be more popular.

Harry Colt was typical of this new breed of golf architect. A lawyer by profession, he was commissioned to design a new course among the sandhills of Rye on the Sussex coast. Rated as one of the best links courses in southern England, it made his reputation and quickly led to other projects at Coombe Hill and The Addington. Soon after, Harry Colt left the law to concentrate on his new career as a golf course designer. Like his many of his contemporaries, Colt concentrated primarily on inland courses incorporating many features like trees, ponds and heather, features that were not found on seaside links. Acknowledged as the master of his profession, Harry Colt designs can be found all around the world: Wentworth (East and West), Sunningdale (New Course), Swinley Forest, St George's Hill, St Andrews (Eden Course), Le Touquet (France), Royal Portrush (Northern Ireland), and the redesigned Muirfield.

As golf's popularity spread to America, one of Colt's associates, Alister MacKenzie, was in the forefront of

Above: *The 10th hole at Old Sunningdale.*

new golf course designers looking to make his fortune. Like Colt had done with his profession, MacKenzie relinquished his former medical practice, turning to golf course architecture full-time. While still in England he had designed Moortown and Alwoodley, and modified Tom Morris's work at Lahinch. Then, before moving to America, he finished the West course at Royal Melbourne in Australia. All four golf courses had been well received and his reputation for visually attractive golf courses preceded him to America.

Below: *The glory of Augusta National, home of the U. S. Masters.*

Above: *The classic 16th hole at Cypress Point.*

Alister MacKenzie's first American commission was on the cliffs above Cypress Point on the Monterey Peninsula in California. The original designer, Seth Raynor, had died suddenly and MacKenzie was given the unenviable task of matching the Pebble Beach course just along the coast. Utilizing the steep cliffs and sloping terrain, he performed his task magnificently. Today, Cypress Point's fifteenth, sixteenth and seventeenth holes on the coastal stretch are among the most photographed golf holes in the world. His work there also led directly to his commission from Bobby Jones to

Below: *A panoramic view of Parque da Florestra.*

design the new Augusta National.

Despite the beautiful heath and heather courses being built in England in the early 1900s, it was in the United States that golf architecture really took off. With designers like Colt and MacKenzie not limited to any particular style, golf courses were laid out on every conceivable type of land. However, this early boom inevitably led to mistakes being made.

In 1895, a newspaperman called Tom Bendelow resigned from his job at the *New York Herald* and turned his hand to golf course design. His sole qualification when he started was that he spoke with a convincing Scottish accent. Working for Spaldings Bros as a 'design-consultant', his golf courses were labelled descriptively as 'Sunday Specials' because of the time it took him to design them. With few clients knowledgeable enough about golf to question his methods, Bendelow would confidently walk around the proposed site, plant one stick for the tee, another for the fairway bunker, and mark the green with a pile of stones. He would repeat this same process nine, twelve or eighteen times, depending on the amount of holes required. The only things left to chance were the greens – whether square or round.

Amazingly, Tom Bendelow perpetrated over six hundred 'Sunday Specials' across America before anyone questioned the Scottish expert on his designs. Even then, he remained steadfastly confident of his own abilities, claiming that more Americans had learned to play golf on a 'Bendelow course' than anywhere else. He was probably right.

America now boasts some of the greatest golf courses in the world. Inspired by the invaluable research of C. B. MacDonald, golf course architecture reached new heights during the early 1900s. Classic courses like Oakmont, Winged Foot, Baltusrol, Pinehurst, Augusta National and Merion were all built during this high renaissance period of American design. Today, the United States still leads the world in innovative golf course design and looks set to do so for the foreseeable future.

The first United States Open Championship was played on 4 October 1895. Staged over the short nine-hole course at Newport, Rhode Island, it played a mere supporting role to the three-day National Amateur tournament held earlier in the same week. Like the inaugural US Amateur Championship, the professional's championship was originally scheduled for the month before, but had been postponed because it clashed with the America's Cup yacht race. When the National Amateur finally did get started, it attracted a good entry of thirty-two golfers and was enthusiastically supported by the rich Rhode island set. The first US Open, by comparison, was played on an empty, garbage-strewn course, with only ten professionals and one amateur attending.

With the carnival atmosphere of the three-day Amateur event nothing more than a distant memory, the 36-hole professional tournament got underway. Played over a single day, the first winner was Horace Rawlins, a nineteen-year-old Englishman who had arrived at Newport Golf Club only eight months before to take up his post as assistant professional. Using hickory shafted clubs and a guttie ball, young Rawlins's

*Left: Fred Herd, winner of the 1898 U. S. Open at Myopia Hunt Club, Mass.*

winning total of 173 not only won him $150 in prize money, but helped to write him into the first page of US Open history. Horace Rawlins defended his title the following year at Shinnecock Hills Golf Club, Long Island, finishing runner-up to Scotsman James Foulis. Unlike Newport, Shinnecock was an attractive eighteen-hole layout, which accounted for the rise in competitors to 35. The tournament still remained an anti-climactic sideshow to the United States Amateur event, but professional interest was growing and so was the prize money.

James Foulis was favorite to win the 1897 event as it was played at his home club of Chicago. The American Association who ran the event bravely attempted to attract more interest by staging the tournament between the semi-final and final of the US Amateur. Foulis himself could do no better than tie for third place behind English professional Joe Lloyd. Lloyd, who spent his winters teaching at Pau in France, worked the rest of the year at the Essex Country Club in Manchester, Massachusetts. Continuing the trend of British-born professionals winning the event, he beat Scotsman Willie Anderson by a single stroke with his two-round total of 162.

The US Open gained its independence in 1898 when the umbilical cord which held it to the National Amateur was finally cut. The tournament itself was extended from 36 to 72 holes in keeping with the British Open which had changed to the longer format six years earlier at Muirfield. Played at the Myopia Hunt Club in South Hamilton, Massachusetts, it was won by yet another exiled Scot, Fred Herd. In what must have been a laborious exercise, Herd, from the Washington Park Club in Chicago, navigated the short nine-hole course eight times for a total of 328. The following year, the US Open made a quick return to the Myopia Hunt Club where Willie

*Below: Willie Anderson (left) shot an 85 to beat Alex Smith (right) in the play-off for the 1901 Open.*

Smith, a transplanted Scot from Carnoustie, won by a record margin of 11 strokes – a record which has yet to be beaten.

The first United States Open of the twentieth century saw the appearance of two great golfing stars from Britain – Harry Vardon and J. H. Taylor. At the time it was vaunted by the American Golf Association that both champions had come specifically to play in the event. The truth was that both Vardon and Taylor were over in the United States on an exhibition tour promoting the latest golfing equipment. Despite this, both men put up a great fight, with Harry Vardon winning with rounds of 79, 78, 76 and 80 for a total of 313 – just two shots ahead of Taylor, who suffered an air-shot on the final green.

Without either Vardon or Taylor in the field for the 1901 event, it became dominated by British-born club professionals. Willie Anderson, who worked at the Pittsfield Country Club in Massachusetts, began his own small period of domination by winning the first US Open play-off. Tied with Alex Smith after four rounds, Anderson captured the eighteen-hole decider by a single stroke with his round of 85. Inspired by his triumph, Willie Anderson went on to win three more championships from 1902 to 1905.

Anderson, despite having made his professional life in the United States, remained a Scottish traditionalist at heart. In the 1902 event, he refused the new Haskell rubber-core ball in favor of the old guttie. With Laurie Auchterlonie from St Andrews winning with four rounds of 78, 78, 74 and 77, it was a mistake he would not make again; at Baltusrol (1903), Glen View, Illinois (1904), and Myopia, South Hamilton (1905), Anderson used the new rubber-core ball. This amazing run of four victories in five years stood as a US Open record until it was finally equalled by Bobby Jones and Ben Hogan a few years later.

Justice was done in the 1907 Championship at Onwentsia Golf Club at Lake Forest, Illinois. Alex Smith, who had finished runner-up to Fred Herd in 1898, lost to Willie Anderson in the 1901 play-off, and in 1905 finally won the championship he craved. Three years later he won again at the Philadelphia Cricket Club, but only after a three-man play-off with Johnny McDermott and Macdonald Smith.

With the exception of Harry Vardon in 1900, the first fifteen years of the United States Open Championship had been dominated by Scottish and English professionals based at American clubs. The desire for a 'home-grown' winner was getting stronger, with the closest to date being Johnny McDermott. McDermott was a brash former caddy who hailed from the Atlantic City Country Club in New Jersey. Losing to Smith in the 1910 play-off had been a great disappointment to him, and he arrived for the 1911 Championship in Chicago in determined mood. Playing aggressively all week, his four-round total of 307 tied him with George Simston and Michael Brady, and another play-off beckoned. The following day, McDermott struggled to an 80, and the United States had its first home winner.

The following year, Johnny McDermott proved his win was no fluke by winning with an excellent score of 294. In 1912, par for the Country Club of Buffalo was set at 74, so his rounds of 75, 74, 74 and 71 made him the first competitor to win the US Open with a sub-par total. And as if McDermott's back-to-back triumphs were not enough, the British stranglehold on the tournament was finally broken for good in 1913.

Francis Ouimet was a skinny, perpetually nervous amateur of twenty years of age. Before the tournament had even started at Brookline, he had considered pulling out after two disastrous practice rounds of 88. Fortunately for him and American golf,

*Below: Ted Ray (playing from the bunker) sensationally beaten by Francis Ouimet in a play-off for the US Open Championship at Brookline in 1913.*

Above: *Johnny McDermott (shown putting) became the first home-grown professional to win the US Open at Chicago in 1911.*

he stayed on and played himself into golf history. As in 1900, Harry Vardon was in the United States playing an exhibition tour, and entered looking for his second title. Unlike before, he was joined by fellow Jerseyman and good friend, Ted Ray. Even with Vardon in the field, the pipe-smoking Ray was considered by many as favorite to win the title. Having already beaten Vardon into second place in the 1912 Open Championship at Muirfield, his form on the American Tour had been outstanding.

Prior to the tournament, the weather at the Country Club in Brookline had been atrocious. No doubt used to these very British conditions, Vardon and Ray rose to the challenge with four-round totals of 304. Out on the course, an unknown professional called Walter Hagen needed to par the final seven holes to get into a play-off. Not surprisingly, his inexperience showed, and Hagen lost his chance. Later in the day, another unknown had the outside chance of forcing a tie. As with Hagen, no one expected him to play the last six holes in two under par, but that is exactly what he did.

American interest in the three-man play-off was tremendous. National newspapers carried the 'David and Goliath' story in banner headlines on the front pages. Millions more waited for the result to be announced. Francis Ouimet himself, the golfer who had generated all this interest, was a regular caddie at Brookline. His caddie for the week and for the play-off was a very serious looking ten-year-old called Eddie Lowery. Half the size of the lanky Ouimet, Lowery would constantly remind his man to 'Keep your eye on the ball'. It was good advice; the timid Ouimet beat his illustrious rivals by five clear shots and created a national sensation. Suddenly golf was no longer regarded as a society sport. On the back of Francis Ouimet's splendid victory, millions of working-class Americans wanted to play the game – overnight, golf had become the sport of the people.

At Midlothian Country Club in 1915, the number of entries soared, prize money was raised, and the United States Open had now superseded the US Amateur as the country's premier tournament. Inspired by Francis Ouimet's performance, America's leading amateurs now sought the big prize, and some of them even succeeded. Following Walter Hagen's first win at Midlothian, a young amateur from Upper Montclair called Jerome D. Travers won in 1915 at Baltusrol. In 1916 the US Open was held at the Minikhada Club in Minneapolis. There, yet another amateur, Charles 'Chick' Evans, triumphed before the tournament itself was suspended during the final two years of World War I.

The post-war years saw the emergence of many of the greats of American golf, including the flamboyant professional Walter Hagen, who won his second title in 1919. Even after Ted Ray

Right: *Walter Hagen at the 1914 US Open at Midlothian Country Club.*

managed to edge out professional Ralph Guldahl. The last amateur to break the professionals' ever-tightening grip on the Championship, he was almost emulated in the late 1930s by the talented Lawson Little. Little, renowned for his match-play rather than stroke-play skills, finally won the US Open in 1940, but only after he had turned professional.

Two years later, the United States Open – like everything else – took second place to the events in Europe and the Far East. As in World War I, tournament play was suspended and golf went into morning for the potential champions it was to lose in six years of war. The US Open, like American golf itself, had come along way from the nine-hole course at Rhode Island in 1895. Golf was now the game of the people, and if a tournament was going to belong to them, then it would have to be the United States Open.

Below: *A portrait of Gene Sarazen. A high school dropout, he became the friend and golfing partner to royalty as well as one of the most respected golf professionals of his era.*

and Harry Vardon made it a British one–two at Inverness in the following year, American golf was on the rise. The tenacious, quick-fire Gene Sarazen burst on to the scene, but then the greatest player of all time, Robert Tyre Jones, was to dominate the US Open as he was to dominate golf in general.

With the retirement of Bobby Jones in 1930, the amateur stranglehold on the US Open had ended. Unable to match the steady week-in, week-out competition and practice, the amateurs gradually fell away. The only exception came in 1933 at North Shore Golf Club in Glen View, Illinois, when Johnny Goodman just

*'The Golfer's Dream' a watercolor painted by Harry Rowntree, circa 1930*

The twenty-year period of calm between the two wars was a time of great social change in Britain. In the immediate post-war era of the 1920s, those who had expected a better way of life after returning to England from the trenches found that very little had changed. Long working hours in poorly paid jobs meant that attitudes hardened. Resentment grew toward the wealthy upper classes, with working-class people no longer content to accept poverty, ill-health and slum housing. The result was widespread civil unrest.

Golf at this time was considered a mainly upper-class sport. Those who had time to play it, and could afford to do so, did it in the privacy and plush surroundings of their exclusive golf clubs. Working-class people were seen on the course but only as caddies and greenkeepers. The humble club professional was allowed to play and give lessons to his members, but under no circumstances was he allowed to socialize in the clubhouse afterwards. Only on the course did he approach any sort of familiarity, but he was expected never to overstep the social boundaries of his class.

Unlike in Scotland, golf in England had come to symbolize differences in class and status. The golfing boom of the late nineteenth century had seen enormous growth in interest in the sport, but many golf clubs still only accepted applications from 'suitable' candidates from the right class and social background. The more established private clubs in England, and especially those in the Home Counties, had a reputation for social snobbery which was probably well deserved. Well-to-do members jealously guarded their privacy and it was made abundantly clear that working-class golfers were not welcome.

Inside these private golf clubs, things were little better. Working-class hirelings like the club professional were tolerated as a necessary evil – he was considered the servant of the

Below: *Captained by Alex Balfour (right) the British Curtis Cup team of 1934 were the first ladies to participate in an international match overseas. Played at Chevy Chase Country Club, they were eventually defeated by the United States by 12 matches to 6.*

Left: 'The
Downtrodden
Professional'
of the early
1920s.

club and was expected to keep his shop open from dawn to dusk. Expected to have a rudimentary knowledge of club repairs, his main task was to supply golf equipment to his members and occasionally give the odd lesson. He was obliged to eat his lunch inside his shop and never, under any circumstances, venture inside the clubhouse. (Even eminent players like Harry Vardon were known to eat outside between rounds, while the amateurs who had admired their golf retired to the clubhouse.)

After 1920, the social changes which were sweeping across Britain finally arrived at the humble pro-shop door. In what was a gradual process, American Walter Hagen is widely credited with raising the social status of the golf professional in the early 1920s. With his refusal to travel second-class, his champagne lifestyle and sartorial elegance, he led the way in breaking down the considerable barriers between amateurs and professionals. There is a famous story about his first Open Championship appearance at Deal in 1920. Arriving at the clubhouse to change into his golfing clothes, Hagen was barred from entering, as were all golf professionals at the time. Told somewhat haughtily to change his

clothes inside the pro-shop with the rest of the competitors, Hagen turned up the next day in a chauffeur-driven limousine. There, in full view of the clubhouse and members, he changed his shoes and served himself champagne from a hamper.

While it was a typically flamboyant gesture from Walter Hagen, it had no real effect in Britain. Hagen had once said: 'I don't want to be a millionaire, I just want to live like one.' Although an admirable ambition in many ways, for the poorly paid British club professional freezing in his shop in winter it was a long way removed from reality. Golf professionals would still remain excluded from the clubhouse for many years to come but at least the first shot had been fired in their long battle for acceptance.

Shortly after the Open Championship at Deal, a far more significant step was taken at Oxhey Golf Club in Hertfordshire. Ted Ray, the club's professional, had just beaten Harry Vardon to win the 1920 US Open Championship at the Inverness Club, Toledo. In honor of his victory, Ted Ray was elected an honorary member of Oxhey. A fairly commonplace event today, back in the 1920s it was considered an unprecedented step to allow a golf professional to become a member of a private club. Although Ray had been British Open Champion in 1912 and was a popular and respected golfer, his appointment caused a great deal of discussion, and

not a little controversy. Finally, when the dust settled, other private clubs saw the benefits of having their own star player as a member. In what became something of a competition, the three most prominent players of the pre-war era, Harry Vardon, J. H. Taylor and James Braid, were all honored by their home clubs. Soon the practice of electing a long-serving club professional to club membership became the norm, and slowly the social barriers began to crumble.

In the Open Championship at Prestwick in 1925, it was suggested for the first time that professionals should be allowed to change

Left: *Walter Hagen (left) and six times British Open champion Harry Vardon.*

inside the clubhouse. It met with strong resistance from some of the older members, but a compromise was finally reached, and changing rooms were given over to the professionals for the week. Despite this allowance, the professionals were still critical of the arrangement and demanded better conditions at future championships. In recognition of the increasing status of the professional golfer, the Royal and Ancient had met with their association and promised action on the matter.

Formed over 20 years before, the Professional Golfers' Association had successfully settled this potentially sensitive issue with great diplomacy. It proved to be the start of closer links between golf's ruling body and the professionals' own representatives. Two years later, in 1927, it would lead to the involvement of the professionals on the potentially sensitive subject of legalizing steel shafts. Established in 1903 to safeguard the interests and welfare of the club professional, the Professional Golfers' Association was conducted along strict trade union lines. As such, it initially found little favor with those pre-war private golf clubs whose members regarded any sort of union membership as little short of Bolshevism.

The PGA also played little part in the promotion of golf tournaments before the war. Apart from the Open Championship, organized tournaments were few in number, and offered little prize money. Exhibition matches between the top players were organized by the clubs themselves, with appearance money paid directly to the players. All this was to change after 1933, with the appointment of retired Royal Navy officer, Commander R. C. T. Roe, as the new PGA Secretary.

Realizing the growing importance of tournament golf in expanding the professionals' status and influence, Commander Roe set about developing an extensive program of regional and national events. Supported by top name players like J. H. Taylor and James Braid, these PGA events proved to be an immediate success with professionals and public alike. As Roe had envisaged, the more that people got to see professionals play, the

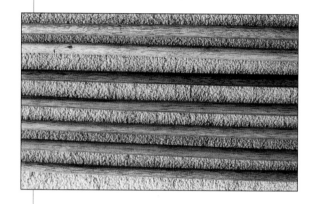

Right: *Moving forward from hickory (below) to the steel shafted clubs of the late 1920s.*

higher their social standing would become. It was a long process, but he was eventually proved right. By the time Commander Roe retired in 1958, tournaments like the *News of the World* PGA Matchplay were well established and the public perception of the golf professional had changed forever.

Another result of the new, more 'modern' outlook on the traditional game was the change from hickory shafts to tubular steel ones.

Wooden shafted golf clubs had been in constant use from the fifteenth century onwards. Originally made from ash and elm, they were superseded over three centuries later by the more resilient wood, hickory. Then in November 1929, the use of steel shafts for golf clubs was finally approved by the R&A Rules of Golf Committee. Following the lead of the United States Golf Association who had legalized them five years earlier, the game of golf had effectively entered the modern era.

The first experimental steel shafts had been introduced in the late 1890s without much success. Unlike the more adventurous golfers of today, the great majority of the golfing public had resisted change, preferring to stay with the more traditional wooden shafts. This resistance to change was sadly typical of

Left: *1920 British Open champion George Duncan.*

golfers down through the years. The guttie ball which ultimately revolutionized the game of golf had been invented in 1848, but it was at least another twenty years before it finally ousted the feather ball.

The same applied to the revolutionary Haskell rubber-core. Ushered in at the turn of the century, it had been roundly criticized for making golf too easy! With public resistance strong, exhibition matches were arranged to try and influence a more positive attitude toward the new ball. Using top professionals like Harry Vardon and James Braid, 'Guttie versus Rubber-core' matches became quite common in the early 1900s. As with the early days of the guttie, opposition was strong, but eventually the traditionalists were won over and the 'Bounding Billy' rubber-core ball was finally accepted. Two decades later, the battle would begin again over steel shafts.

Despite being in limited use some years before, steel shafts were not made legal in the United States until 1924. Failing to grip the public imagination, they were considered too gimmicky by the top players of the day. They were thought to help beginners obtain more distance with their drives, but for tournament play they were inconsistent and unreliable. While matched sets of hickory-shafted clubs all performed within a given range, steel shafts could be either too flexible or not flexible enough.

The first major manufacturer of steel shafts in Britain was Accles & Pollock. They had pioneered the first tubular shaft as early as 1913, but were unable to develop it further because of the advent of World War I. Shortly after, they joined forces with the American Fork & Hoe Manufacturing Company, which eventually became the True Temper Corporation. So when steel shafts were finally legalized in the United States and later in Britain, Accles & Pollock were among the first to go into mass-production.

By the time steel shafts were legalized in Britain, True Temper in the United Stated had improved their consistency. With better quality steel shafts, leading professionals like Tommy Armour and Gene Sarazen now used iron shafts in their clubs. In Britain, the first matched sets of steel-shafted clubs were introduced around 1930. They were coated in a brown

Above: *Edward VIII was known for his love of golf. Here, as the Prince of Wales, he follows play in the 1930 Walker Cup match at Sandwich.*

wood-grained plastic to lessen golfers' fears about their novelty and gimmickiness. Soon the more adventurous golfers had steel shafts fitted into their drivers. Most still preferred wooden shafts in their irons, but as with the introduction of carbon-graphite shafts today, things were slowly beginning to change.

Another effect of the steel shaft was the subtle changes in golfers' technique. The swing became more rounded and smoother, with less of the big forearm smash associated with J. H. Taylor and George Duncan. Smooth swingers like Henry Cotton, Bobby Locke and Sam Snead all mastered this new technique and benefited from it with Open Championship victories in the 1930s and 1940s. They had the foresight to see the changes that steel shafts would bring and adapted accordingly. The success of British players like Henry Cotton brought a grudging acceptance of steel-shafted clubs and by the mid-1940s they were in common use. The five hundred-year reign of the wooden shaft was finally over and the modern era had begun.

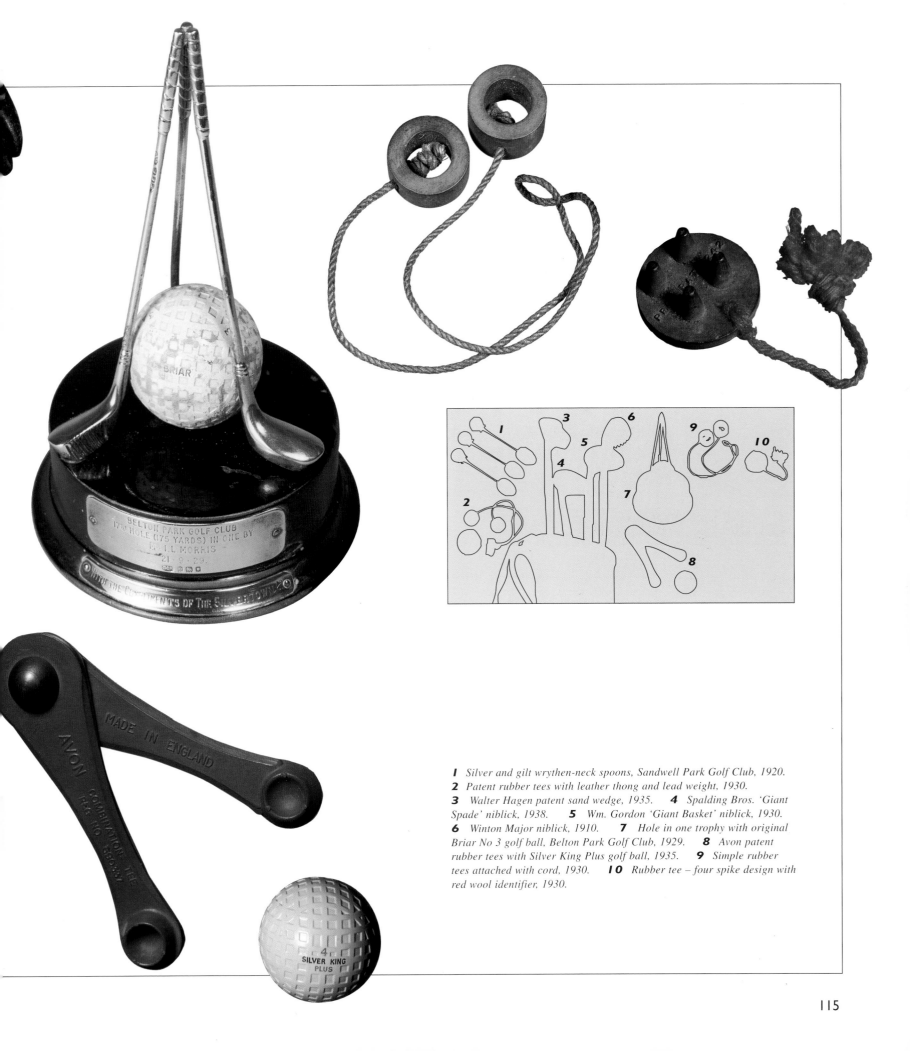

1  Silver and gilt wrythen-neck spoons, Sandwell Park Golf Club, 1920.
2  Patent rubber tees with leather thong and lead weight, 1930.
3  Walter Hagen patent sand wedge, 1935.  4  Spalding Bros. 'Giant Spade' niblick, 1938.  5  Wm. Gordon 'Giant Basket' niblick, 1930.
6  Winton Major niblick, 1910.  7  Hole in one trophy with original Briar No 3 golf ball, Belton Park Golf Club, 1929.  8  Avon patent rubber tees with Silver King Plus golf ball, 1935.  9  Simple rubber tees attached with cord, 1930.  10  Rubber tee – four spike design with red wool identifier, 1930.

Above: *Jim Barnes, one of the few to have won both the British and United States Open Championships.*

Below right: *J. Douglas Edgar, losing finalist in the 1920 US P.G.A Championship.*

The first United Stated PGA Championship was played at the Siwanoy Country Club in Bronxville, New York, on 10–14 October 1916. Backed by department store heir Rodman Wanamaker of Philadelphia, it was based on the prestigious *News of the World* matchplay tournament in England. Within weeks of the first American Professional Golfers' Association being formed, it was Wanamaker himself who proposed that ordinary club professionals should have a tournament of their own.

Back in 1916 this was a huge step to take. The gentlemen amateurs that effectively ran American golf at the turn of the century had inherited much of the same social snobbery of their British counterparts. The US Amateur Championship was considered the blue riband event of American golf, with the professionals' US Open relegated to an insignificant sideshow. Despite

the crowds that flocked to see Harry Vardon on his rare exhibition tours of America, the typical golf professional was seen very much as a second-class citizen. With the club professional not permitted to enter the clubhouse where they worked, the United States Professional Golfers' Association was established to protect their rights and raise their social standing. Following the example of the British PGA which had been in existence since 1902, the new Association had taken Wanamaker's suggestion and inaugurated the first Championship in the hope that it would raise the public profile of their members.

Billed as 'The Championship of the Professional Golfers' Association of America', the eventual winner would get a cash prize, a trophy and a gold medal. A silver medal would go to the runner-up, while third place would have one in bronze. The total prize fund of $2,580 was supplied by Rodman Wanamaker with the 32 professionals taken from regional qualifying rounds played a week earlier. The first winner was 'Long Jim' Barnes, a 30-year-old native of Lelant, Cornwall. In the closely fought 36-hole final, he just managed to edge out another expatriate British professional, Jock Hutchison, one up.

With the outbreak of World War I, the Championship Cup stayed with John Barnes for four years. With competitive golf suspended, no tournaments were played between 1917 and 1918. Then in 1919 Barnes successfully defended his title against Fred McLeod at the Engineers Country Club in Roslyn, New York. Jock Hutchison who had lost in the first final to Barnes, finally won the trophy in 1920. Even then, he had to enter the tournament as a reserve, having failed to qualify in the regional competition. In yet another close final, the diminutive Scotsman beat J. Douglas Edgar on the final hole to win the Championship trophy, gold winner's medal and $500 in prize money.

Hutchison's victory effectively ended an era. The first three PGA Championships had been won by British professionals who had migrated to America for work. In 1921, Walter Hagen, a cocky ex-caddie from Rochester, New York, became the first American-born professional to win the title at Inwood Country Club, Far Rockaway, in New York. Hagen, who had been beaten by Jock Hutchison in the semi-final of the inaugural event, had demolished his opponents on his way to the final. Scoring a fine 69 in the morning round of the final, his three and two victory over 'Long Jim' Barnes, heralded the beginning of what has been called the 'Hagen era'. During a period of unprecedented domination, he won five PGA Championships in seven years, rising from a virtual unknown to become the most successful professional in American golf. It was probably Walter Hagen more than anyone else who helped the US PGA achieve their goal of raising the public perception of the golf professional. With his flamboyant lifestyle and charismatic charm, he imbued the game with a dash of color which put golf on to the back pages of every newspaper in America.

Left: *The distinctive follow-through of Gene Sarazen. Starting as a caddy, he became the first winner of all four major championships open to professionals.*

Left: *Record gallery watches Tommy Armour hole the winning putt on the 18th green in the 1927 United States Open at Oakwood.*

Despite his early dominance of the event, Walter Hagen had an increasingly strong rival in the shape of a youngster called Gene Sarazen. Destined to become a golfing legend himself, he won his first PGA Championship in 1922. Walter Hagen had chosen to play in the British Open at Sandwich rather than defend his PGA title at Oakmont. Taking advantage of his absence, this confident twenty-year-old youngster straight out of caddy ranks beat Emmett French in the final to win his first major championship. With Hagen back the following year at Pelham Country Club, it was expected that he would pick up where he had left off. Meeting in the final, the young Sarazen surprised everyone by beating his illustrious rival one up in a closely fought battle which went all the way to the 38th hole.

Sarazen, whose Italian immigrant family name was Saraceni, was a stocky, hard-hitting golfer with a keen mind and abundance of natural charm. Only 5 feet 5 inches in height, he was one of the élite band of professionals to have ever won all four major titles in different years – US Open (1922 and 1932), British Open (1932), US Masters (1935), USPGA (1922, 1923 and 1933). His record for longevity and match-play victories is also the best in the tournament's history. Gene Sarazen, who celebrated his ninety-second birthday in 1994, played in 29 PGA Championships and won 59 matches – eleven more than his nearest rival, Walter Hagen. Together with Hagen he was one of five men to dominate the first fifteen years of the tournament. The other players were Jim Barnes (1916, 1919), Jock Hutchison (1920), Leo Diegel (1928, 1929) and Tommy Armour (1930).

In the late 1930s the United States PGA Championship saw the emergence of some of the great players of the post-war era like Byron Nelson and Sam Snead. The elegant Texan Byron Nelson had already lost in the 1939 final to Henry Picard at

Pomonok, before beating Sam Snead one year later at Hershey Country Club. One of American golf's most prolific winners of professional tournaments, his record between 1939 to 1945 totals two championship wins (1940 and 1945) and three losing final appearances (1939, 1941 and 1945).

Snead had also lost a final to Paul Runyan in 1938 before going on to win the last Championship before the war in 1942 – beating Jim Turnesa two and one at Seaview, Atlantic City. Despite there being only a one-year suspension for the war, many other PGA Champions of the 1930s failed to make any impression after 1943. Players like two-times winners Denny Shute and Paul Runyon, John Revolta and Vic Ghezzi – all great players in their day – have passed quietly into the tournament's pre-war history.

Despite its glorious past, the United States PGA has been relegated in recent years to the status of the 'fourth major'. The final major championship of the season after the Masters, the British Open and United States Open, it sadly pales in comparison with its more prestigious and exalted rivals. The Championship itself lost its match-play format in 1958, becoming a standard 72-hole stroke-play event. Perhaps from that moment on the United States PGA Championship lost its uniqueness and suffered a downfall in popularity. The post-war years have not been kind to the professionals' own tournament.

The dramatic 36-hole finals of the past are now long dead, sacrificed on the altar of modern-day television coverage. But with the excitement and drama of the Ryder Cup series enthralling millions every two years, the demand for more match-play events is growing ever stronger. Golf has always been about development and change, so perhaps one day the professionals' own championship will revert back to its original format. Until then, it will have to live on the glories of its past.

Left: *Sam Snead, losing finalist in 1938 and 1940, beat Jim Turnesa to record his first US P.G.A. championship title in 1942.*

In June 1926, Samuel A. Ryder was enjoying a quiet drink in Wentworth clubhouse. Outside on the West Course, top British players were limbering up for a tournament which also included a sprinkling of American professionals. As the St Albans seed merchant sat with his friends, he watched thoughtfully as the players came in after their round. Conversation turned to the forthcoming Open Championship at Royal Lytham St Annes. The friends speculated whether it would be a home-grown player who would win, or possibly another American.

The argument was thrown back and forth, debating the individual merits of British and American golfers; certainly Walter Hagen was favorite but what about George Duncan and Ted Ray? It was all typical clubhouse speculation, but it sparked an idea in the mind of Sam Ryder. In typically positive fashion he suggested an informal match be arranged between the American and British professionals. The idea was put to the players, and with Hagen agreeing enthusiastically on behalf of the Americans, the match was planned for the next day.

The following day at Wentworth, the first unofficial Ryder Cup began. The British team began well by winning all four morning foursome matches, while in the afternoon past British Open Champion George Duncan beat Walter Hagen in the top

*Below: George Duncan against Walter Hagen in the Ryder Cup singles at Moortown, Leeds, in 1929.*

singles match. With the rest of his team performing equally well, all that stopped a complete American debacle was 'Wild' Bill Mehlhorn's win over Archie Compston and Emmet French's half with Ernie Whitcombe. The final result was a resounding victory to the British – thirteen-and-a-half to one-and-a-half.

At the small celebration which followed, Duncan suggested to Sam Ryder that he should consider making the match a regular event – perhaps even offer a trophy. Impressed by the spirit of friendship shown by both teams, Ryder agreed and shortly after contacted the relevant American and British Professional Golfers' Associations for their approval. The graceful gold trophy which is still played for today was designed with the small figure of Abe Mitchell standing proudly on top – a sign of the respect in which Sam Ryder held his former golfing tutor. Taking over a year to make, the trophy was not actually ready until the second match at Moortown, but to all intents and purposes the Ryder Cup was born.

The first of the biennial matches was scheduled for 3–4 June 1927, at the Worcester Country Club in Massachusetts. The cost of sending the British team to the United States had been raised through an appeal launched by George Philpot, Editor of *Golf Illustrated*. Philpot, who also doubled as team manager, joined the players in Southampton for the five-day sea-crossing to New York. Seeing the team off, Sam Ryder wished them well but his lifelong fear of sea journeys meant that he did not make the trip himself. Shortly after boarding the *Aquitania*, British morale

suffered a major blow when team captain Abe Mitchell was struck down with appendicitis. Ryder wrote to his great friend declaring: 'Let us hope our team can win, but it is the play without the Prince of Denmark.'

In New York harbor, waiving all customs formalities, the British team were greeted by brass bands and speeches from the city mayor. Accompanied by a motorcycle escort, they were then whisked away in a fleet of chauffeur-driven limousines through downtown Manhattan to their luxury hotel. In the days that preceded the actual match, banquets and champagne receptions were put on in their honor, with New York society turning out to welcome them to America. Coming from the austere, depressed Britain of the 1920s, many of the working-class British players were completely overwhelmed by this extravagant display of American hospitality.

Possibly as a result, the British Ryder Cup team were totally overwhelmed and overpowered – unfortunately on the course as well as off it!

With the match played over four foursome matches and eight singles, the Americans were desperate to revenge the defeat at Wentworth. Inspired by their charismatic captain Walter Hagen, they won three foursomes and six singles, to run out eventual winners at nine-and-a-half to two-and-a-half. Despite George Duncan's win over Joe Turnesa in the singles, it was a desper-

ately disappointing result for the British and their thoughts quickly turned to Moortown in two years' time.

The second Ryder Cup match was played on 27–28 April 1929. Once again, the Americans took the early initiative, winning the foursome matches two-and-a-half to one-and-a-half. With the eight singles to come, it looked like being yet another American triumph. An infamous tale has been passed down through the years on Hagen's reaction to being drawn against Duncan in the singles. 'Well boys,' the flamboyant American is supposed to have told his team-mates, 'that's a sure point for us.' George Duncan must have got wind of his opponent's rash boast because the following day he crushed Walter Hagen by the astounding margin of ten and eight! With Compston also beating Sarazen, and losses for Watrous, Farrell and Turnesa, it left a shell-shocked American team wondering what they had done to upset the British. With the final result seven to five to the home side, British pride was restored, and it left the series tied at one each.

In December that year, Samuel Ryder handed over his elegant trophy to the British PGA. Rather than presenting it to the Royal

*Above: Rival captains Walter Hagen (USA) and Ted Ray of Great Britain (with pipe) talking before the first 'official' Ryder Cup match at Worcester Country Club in 1927.*

*Below: Abe Mitchell drawing off the 15th tee in the 1929 Open Championship at Muirfield. The personal tutor of Sam Ryder, it is his image that adorns the top of the famous gold trophy.*

Above: *Played on American soil for the first time, the winning US Ryder Cup team pose with the trophy after narrowly defeating the British side.*

Below: *George Duncan playing in the Open Championship qualifying round at Muirfield in 1929.*

and Ancient, he felt that the professionals themselves were the best people to administer future Ryder Cups, and signed a Deed of Trust to that effect.

Thus the series was underway, played every two years with the venue alternating between Britain and the United States. From the comparative cold of Yorkshire, the 1931 Ryder Cup was played at Scioto Country Club in Columbus, in the boiling heat of an American summer. With temperatures permanently in the high nineties, British team manager Fred Pignon described the problems his players were facing: 'In this weather golf is not a game, it is a form of torture.' Apart from the searing heat, British morale had already been dented by the loss of Henry Cotton over a petty squabble concerning traveling arrangements.

Cotton's absence was a double-edged sword for Fred Pignon. Considered standoffish by some of his fellow team members, Cotton's often outrageous demands for better accommodation and money had not improved team morale. On the other hand, he was openly acknowledged as the best British prospect for years and was desperately needed against a strong American side. Even before the Ryder Cup at Moortown, Henry Cotton's maverick attitude had been a constant source of

irritation to the PGA. Excluded from the Ryder Cup match of 1933 because of Sam Ryder's provision that all British players should be resident in Britain (Cotton was a professional at Royal Waterloo in Belgium), and also missing out in 1935 at Ridgewood, New Jersey, because of yet another clash with authority, Henry Cotton was at best an infrequent supporter of the Ryder Cup cause.

Almost inevitably, the Ryder Cup match at Scioto was lost before if had even begun. Walter Hagen repayed his crushing defeat at the hands of George Duncan by beating him and

Arthur Havers ten and nine in the foursomes, partnered by Densmore Shute. The following day, Hagen was jokingly handed a Martini on the first tee of his singles match with Charlie Whitcombe. Hagen smiled, drank his cocktail, then smashed a perfect drive down the middle of the opening fairway. His win over the Englishman in the singles contributed to the American team's nine to three victory.

The history of the Ryder Cup has been littered with close results and heart-stopping final days, but one of the best came at Southport and Ainsdale in 1933. J. H. Taylor was non-playing team captain, and immediately ordered a strict fitness regime for his players which involved early morning workouts on Southport Sands. When the match started, a record crowd swarmed over the sandhills to see them take on the Americans, including the heir to the English throne, Edward, Prince of Wales.

Victory in the foursomes left Britain needing to share the singles to win. A well-balanced match see-sawed all afternoon, first to the Americans, then to the British. Finally, the whole outcome of the Ryder Cup rested on the final singles between Syd Easterbrook and Denny Shute. In scenes reminiscent of later matches at the Belfry, Shute missed from three feet and Easterbrook calmly holed out for an historic win. At the presentation later, the Prince summed up the feelings of everyone when he said: 'In giving this Cup I am naturally impartial, but of course, we are very pleased to have won.'

If Southport in 1933 was a high point for Great Britain, then the 1935 match at Ridgewood, New Jersey, was a depressing low. With press criticism ringing in their ears for a catalogue of inept individual performances, the British side ran out nine to three losers. This defeat was followed at Royal Birkdale by another – the first British defeat on home soil.

Even before the ten-year break for the war, the balance of golfing power had shifted inexorably in favor of the United States. The fledgling American Tour was producing increasingly dedicated full-time professionals, while Britain remain locked in the club servant mentality of the 1920s. As a result, in the sixteen Ryder matches from 1937 to 1977, Britain would only win once, at Lindrick, in 1957.

Above: *The legendary Walter Hagen playing out of a bunker on the 4th hole at Muirfield, on his way to winning the 1929 Open Championship.*

Traditionalists bemoan the modern-day battles between Europe and America, but they forget that by the late 1970s the Ryder Cup was dying of imbalanced competition. Today, the teams are well matched, and interest in the event is greater than ever before. Even allowing for the occasional display of competitive exuberance, the match is played in a spirit of professional friendship which old Sam Ryder would have heartily approved of.

Right: *Bobby Jones competing in the Gold Vase competition at Sunningdale in 1930. By the end of the year he would have achieved the 'Grand Slam' of golf.*

**B**obby Jones came as close to golfing perfection as it is possible to achieve. Remaining an amateur throughout his entire career, he competed against and consistently beat some of the greatest professionals the game has ever known. Blessed with a smooth, rhythmic golf swing and flawless putting stroke, Jones amassed thirteen major titles between 1923 and 1930, including five US Amateurs, four US Opens, three British Opens and one British Amateur title. But the achievement for which he will always be remembered was his legendary 'Grand-slam' of 1930 – a clean sweep of all four major titles in one year, amateur and professional. During his own lifetime and for over half a century since, Jones had been the yardstick against which all other great golfers are measured.

Robert Tyre Jones Jnr was born on 17 March 1902, in Atlanta, Georgia. Named after his straightlaced grandfather, his first introduction to golf came in the summer of 1907, when his family moved to a boarding house near the East Lake course just outside Atlanta. Despite both parents being keen golfers, there was little indication that Bobby would have an athletics career of any kind. Born with an oversized head and frail body, he had a digestive illness that left him eating soft foods until he was five years old. At six, the local children arranged a birthday party for him which included a six-hole mini-golf. Jones himself later admitted that the 'birthday party invitational tournament' was the starting point for his lifelong love affair with the game.

By 1916, the fourteen-year-old Bobby Jones was already looked upon as a child prodigy. The same year, he entered his first US Amateur Championship at the Merion Cricket Club in Philadephia. With a pre-qualifying round before the actual match-play section, Jones's excellent score of 74 created a minor sensation, with his steady progress through the championship itself adding considerably to his growing reputation.

Early in 1922, Bobby Jones had a leg operation, but the enforced rest seemed to improve his form. He finished tied for second place behind Gene Sarazen in the US Open at Chicago, but despite entering the National Amateur at Brookline in con-

Above: *Jones, aged fourteen, playing his first US Amateur Championship at Merion.*
Below: *Bobby Jones (seated centre) pictured with the 1928 US Walker Cup team.*

and he finished the last three holes five, five and six, against par of four, four and four. Jones was disconsolate.

He was, however, given a temporary reprieve. First round rival Hutchison had fallen away, but another contender, Bobby Cruickshank, had sank an eight-foot putt on the final green to tie Jones on 296. In the exciting play-off, both men played to the top of their form. First Jones took the lead, then Cruickshank edged ahead and only three holes were halved all day. Coming down the final fairway, Cruickshank had played short of the large lake guarding the eighteenth green. Jones, who had played this hole so badly only the day before, had the choice – play safe or gamble for victory.

If ever one shot influenced golf history, it was this one. Jones jerked out his long-iron and ripped the ball two hundred yards through the air to within six feet of the hole. To the tremendous roar of the gallery, Bobby Jones tapped in for a 76 and a two-stroke victory. At last he was a champion.

If the first seven years of Bobby Jones's career can be described as famine, the next seven were certainly feast. By the time he next returned to Britain in 1926, he had won two National Amateur titles, at Merion in 1924 and at Oakmont in 1925, as well as being runner-up in the US Open at Oakland Hills and Worcester Country Club in the same year. Despite this enviable record, Jones's consecutive second-place positions in the National Open still led the American press and public to question his ability to win under pressure. Jones was to answer his critics in Britain.

fident form, he was destroyed eight and seven by the eventual winner, Jess Sweetser. Still only twenty, Jones had just graduated from Georgia Tech, and had enrolled at Havard seeking his MA degree. His whole life stretched out before him, but all he could think of was a record of seven years, eleven major tournaments, and still not one victory.

Inwood Country Club, the scene of the 1923 US Open, was a tough par-72 with tight, tree-lined fairways. Bobby Jones fired an opening 71 to find himself just one shot behind leader Jock Hutchison. After three rounds Jones was leading but late on in the final round his play fell to pieces. Instead of playing safely Jones started to press, looking for that final knockout blow. Whether it was the pressure, or his desperate desire to win his first title, his game cracked

Bobby Jones had been looking forward to the British leg of the Walker Cup for five years. In his previous trip as a brash youngster of nineteen, he had not only performed badly but had disgraced himself at the 'Home of Golf' by storming off the Old Course during the 1921

Open. Determined to show his British fans the reformed Robert T. Jones, his behavior was exemplary throughout the whole trip – as was his golf.

After the war, Bobby Jones returned to playing national golf tournaments. In 1919 he tied for second in the Canadian Open and was runner-up in the US Amateur at Oakmont.

In 1920 Jones made his first attempt at the United States Open Championship in Chicago creditably, Bobby Jones finished tied eighth behind Ted Ray.

Jones made his first trip to Britain in 1921 as the youngest member of the American Walker Cup side. As was customary, he also played in the Amateur and Open Championships, but other than helping his team beat the British, he played badly in both. In the Amateur at Hoylake, he lost in the fourth round, while in the Open at St Andrews he tore his card up in the third round after a run of bad holes – a reaction he then regretted all his life. Returning home, he improved a little in the US Open by finishing fifth behind Jim Barnes, but blew up again in the National Amateur where once again he lost in an early round. Having been tipped as a potential championship winner, even Jones himself was beginning to have his doubts.

Despite playing sub-par golf in the British Amateur at Muirfield, Jones eventually lost in the sixth round to Andrew Jamieson. At St Andrews during the Walker Cup, he contributed two good wins to help his American side retain the trophy, but as he headed for Royal Lytham St Annes for the Open, his game was getting even better. In the Open qualifying rounds at Sunningdale, Jones had played what has later been described as the perfect round. Over this leafy Berkshire course with its lightning fast greens and gun-barrel fairways, he scored a six-under-par round of 66, without either a five or a two on his card.

Winning the Open must have seemed an anti-climax after that, but win it he did. With fellow American Al Watrous in second place, Jones had captured the hearts of everyone with his smooth rhythmic swing and gutsy performance. On his

Left: *Roger Wethered, runner-up in the 1921 Open Championship,*

Above: *Jones completes his Grand Slam by winning the US Amateur at Merion in 1930.*

return to the States, he was awarded a ticker-tape parade down Broadway and a congratulatory speech by the Mayor on the steps of New York City Hall.

Almost before the paper had been swept away, Bobby Jones was again in action at the US Open at Sciota Country Club in

Below: *Bobby Jones parades through the streets of New York after winning the 1926 British Open title.*

Left: *Bobby Jones talking to Ben Sayers before the 1921 Open at St Andrews.*

Columbus, Ohio. Huge crowds turned out to watch him make it an Open double – British and American. He did not disappoint them, beating Joe Turnesa into second place. It was the prelude to the most successful period of his life. One year later, he repeated his British Open triumph with a second win at St Andrews. Later the same year, Jones was mixing practice shots with law books as he studied at Emory University. Despite finishing in a stale eleventh place in the US Open at Oakmont he gathered himself to flatten Chick Evans eight and seven in the final of the National Amateur. But as remarkable as his record in recent major tournaments had been, it was nothing compared to 1930.

Having established a busy law practice, Jones came to Britain in 1930 as Captain of the American Walker Cup team. He was also the current holder of the US Open – a title he won in a play-off with Al Espinosa, after sinking a huge putt on the 72nd green at Winged-Foot just to tie.

The Amateur Championship was played over the Old Course at St Andrews, and after some narrow escapes in the early rounds, Jones eventually conquered Roger Wethered seven and six in the final. Despite beating a British player, the huge crowds mobbed the popular American, and a police escort was needed to convey him back to the clubhouse.

The same scenes greeted him at Hoylake for the Open Championship. Starting off with rounds of 70 and 72, he stumbled with two closing rounds of 75–74 for 291. Waiting in the clubhouse, he had to sweat it out as MacDonald Smith and Leo Diegel made strong final round challenges. Ultimately, they both fell two strokes short of tying Jones, and he sailed back to the United States with half of the impossible 'Grand Slam' under his belt.

If Francis Ouimet had lit the flame of golf interest, then Bobby Jones started the bonfire. Golf fever hit new heights in America and thousands of people gathered at New York harbor to welcome him home. Ten thousand more swamped the sunbaked fairways of the Interlachen Course, Minneapolis, to watch him challenge for the US Open title. Under intense pressure from the silver-haired Tommy Armour and the in-form MacDonald Smith, Jones played phenomenal golf. On the final green he had to hole a 50-foot putt for a struggling final round of 75. It was just good enough to beat MacDonald Smith by two, with Armour taking third place.

Shortly after, United Stated Amateur was played at Merion Cricket Club, in the suburbs of Philadelphia. Eighteen thousand fans turned out for the Final against Eugene Homans. Probably the only person amongst millions worldwide who did not want Bobby Jones to win, he competed well before wilting under fierce media pressure. In what turned out to be the easiest of the four legs, Bobby Jones beat Eugene Homans eight and seven to win the only Grand Slam in golf history.

Thus the spectacular career of Robert Tyre Jones Jnr had come full circle. Even today, it is impossible to gauge what an achievement it really was. Modern golfing scholars scoff at the two match-play tournaments that made up the 1930 'Slam'. They also point out the lack of competition for Jones during that era, but great champions are great champions no matter what era. 'If he had come along fifteen or twenty years later, he would still have been the best', it was said.

The United States Masters tournament is all about tradition. Held each spring at the exclusive Augusta National Golf Club in Georgia, it remains a privately run event for a small, select number of golf professionals. In keeping with the high ideals of the club's founder Bobby Jones, it has an enviable reputation for quality and efficiency. The only one of golf's four majors played at the same venue each year, the beauty of Augusta's azalea-lined fairways have captivated golfers worldwide for over sixty years. Born decades after the two big Opens – the British and American – the Masters has risen to challenge these older, more established fixtures as the most prestigious test in golf.

Apart from being the original inspiration for the Masters tournament, Bobby Jones was also the driving force behind the Augusta National Golf Club. After competing his legendary Grand Slam of 1930, he shocked the golfing world by announcing his retirement from big-time competition. Though still only 28, Jones had no intention of giving up the game that had been his life. Content to stay out of the tournament spotlight, he concentrated his efforts on a wider range of golfing projects. He joined A. G. Spalding, helping to design the next generation of golf equipment. He also filmed a series of instructional movie shorts for Warner Brothers as well as broadcasting his own radio show. Bobby Jones was now slowly achieving all his ambitions, but he still had one particular project in mind.

While visiting the small Georgia town of Augusta late in 1930, Jones had met with New York banker, Clifford Roberts, who often vacationed there. Sharing a natural love of golf they became close friends. Discussing the great courses they had both played, Jones confided his longheld desire to build the perfect golf course. Situated somewhere in the heart of the South, this 'dream' course would incorporate some of the great holes that he had played on during his tournament career. Roberts became keenly interested in the idea, suggesting a particular piece of land just west of Augusta that might be suitable. Intrigued by Clifford Robert's description, they went to look at the site shortly after on a cold, December morning. Bobby Jones took one look and knew it would be perfect.

Left: *The natural glory of Bobby Jones' masterpiece: Augusta National Golf Club.*

Originally an old indigo plantation known as Fruitlands, the land had been bought by a Belgian nobleman in 1857 and turned into a nursery. He had planted magnolia seeds along the drive that led to his mansion and let his horticultural flair run wild over the rest of the 365-acre site. Apart from establishing a forest of stately pines, he had introduced a veritable garden wonderland of camellia, azalea and dogwood. Jones later remarked: 'Frankly, I was overwhelmed by the exciting possibilities of a golf course set in the midst of such a nursery.'

The decision made, Jones and Roberts set about turning their dream into a reality. With property prices hit by the Depression, they bought the land at a good price. Canvassing rich friends, a holding company was set up and plans mapped out for the formation of a private club. Membership was by invitation only, with a maximum of thirty coming from the Augusta area. The joining fee was put at $350, with the annual fee of $60.

Left: *Alister MacKenzie, co-designer of Augusta National Golf Club.*

With the Augusta National Golf Club now reality, the respected Scottish golf architect, Alister MacKenzie, was invited to join Bobby Jones in laying out the actual course. Having spent many hours walking over his imaginary golf holes, Jones already had a clear idea of what he wanted. In his initial discussions with MacKenzie, Jones was adamant that as much as possible of the original nursery should be retained, including trees, shrubs and flowers. He maintained that it should be as scenic as possible. Strongly in favor of penalizing the golfer around the greens rather than off the tee, his idea was to have broad, uncluttered fairways which gave the thoughtful golfer several lines of attack. Jones also disliked prohibitively long par-fives and pressed for shorter, more strategic holes where accuracy rather than brute strength was rewarded.

Work began in the spring of 1931 and finished eighteen months later in the fall of 1932. Alister MacKenzie later described Augusta National as 'my finest achievement'. In a design that was considered revolutionary in the 1930s, the course had wide fairways, massive undulating greens and less than 22 bunkers at a time when most championship venues had over 200. Sadly, MacKenzie died shortly after the club was established and never had the opportunity to see his great course put to the test. A white, colonial-style mansion was built at the clubhouse, with a tree-lined driveway leading up to the front entrance, while a rear balcony overlooked the ninth and eighteenth greens. Ed Dudley was appointed the first professional and Augusta National Golf Club was born.

Designed purely and simply as a private members' course, there was never any intention of using it for professional tournaments. Jones himself had always wanted it to be a place where friends got together to play golf in beautiful surroundings, but the fame of Augusta began to spread far beyond the southern heartlands.

By the early 1930s, interest in golf had declined. Bobby Jones's sudden retirement from the game had left a void which not even the charismatic Gene Sarazen could fill. The American public who had taken golf to their hearts in 1930 associated the game entirely with Jones, and in their minds without Jones there was no game. The first professional tour was struggling to make any impression, with only a limited number able to make a living from it. Golf desperately needed a boost. It needed a professional tournament in the South, in 'Bobby Jones country'.

The first person to raise the subject was textile tycoon Fielding Wallace. As well as being active in the US Golf Association, later serving as President, Wallace was also a charter member of Augusta National. In late 1932, he proposed that the US Open should be held at Augusta, and presented his idea to the membership for approval. It was rejected unanimously, but then came the suggestion that perhaps the club itself could put on its own tournament. After much debate, it was finally agreed and plans were quickly put in motion for Augusta's first professional event. A strictly invitation only event, the field would be drawn from the greatest players in the game. It would include all past winners of the United States Amateur and Open titles still living, plus the leading 24 players from the previous year's US Open at North

Left: *Bobby Jones (driving) playing with Walter Hagen in the 1934 US Masters.*

Above: *Winner of the first US Masters, Horton Smith.*

Shore. The tournament would be played on the final weekend in March 1934, over 72 holes of medal play, one round each day for four days. The prize fund of $5,000 would be supplied by the Augusta members and the tournament would be called the Augusta National Invitation. Clifford Roberts had suggested the title 'Masters', but Bobby Jones vetoed the idea on the grounds that it sounded too pompous.

Roberts had also insisted that Jones should play in his own event to help guarantee its popularity. Jones flatly refused, stating that he had determined never to play competitive golf again after 1930. 'I then pointed out to him,' said Roberts many years later, 'that as host, he couldn't very well invite his golfing friends to come and play his course and then not play himself.' Jones finally relented, agreeing to play at least until the tournament had established itself.

At 10.00 am on Thursday 22 March the legendary Robert T. Jones Jnr stepped on to the first tee at Augusta. The gallery numbered over one thousand, and they all followed Jones. Since the news broke about his tournament comeback, the American newspapers and public had talked of little else. High excitement swept the golfing world, and for the first time in four long years, golf was front-page news. Still aged only 32, Bobby Jones had played well in practice, scoring a 65, but the day before the first round, things began to go wrong; although

he used a replica of the famed 'Calamity Jane' putter he had donated to the Royal and Ancient Golf Club Museum, he struggled desperately to find his putting touch. Playing erratically in the pro–amateur event, Jones went into the tournament lacking any degree of confidence whatsoever.

Unsteady with his short game, lacking the radar accuracy of his iron shots of only four years before and partnering a youthful Paul Runyan, Jones three-putted three of the last five greens to finish with an opening score of 76 – 4 over par. The second round saw little improvement. Playing into a freezing wind all day, Jones ended with a 74, including one missed putt from ten inches. With a 36-hole total of 150, the legendary Grand Slammer was eight shots behind halfway leader Horton Smith. Despite putting better for a third round 72, Jones now found himself ten shots behind the gentle giant Smith.

The final day was filled with nostalgia, as Jones was partnered with the great Walter Hagen for the last round. Hagen, now 42, was coming to the end of his own playing career, and after having been in contention after the opening day, had fallen back badly. Bobby Jones had 72, while Hagen rocketed to 77. The tournament itself had a close finish with five players battling it out down the final stretch including the 'home-pro' Ed Dudley. Eventually, the halfway leader Horton Smith finally triumphed by a single stroke with his score of 70-70-70-74 for a winning total of 284.

Four years in the making, Augusta National Golf Club and its invitational tournament were declared resounding successes by players and press alike. In the second year its reputation for producing spectacular finishes was further enhanced by Gene Sarazen's famed double eagle on the fifteenth hole in the final round. Going on to beat Craig Wood in the first 36-hole play-off, Sarazen put his name on the rollcall of Masters winners that now reads like a 'Who's Who' of golfing greats.

Sadly, Bobby Jones to whom Augusta owes everything, died in December 1971 of a crippling spinal disease. While his individual place in golf history is assured, the permanent legacy of the Augusta National and the Masters tournament played over it each spring, will leave golf in his debt forever.

The period between the two wars saw the emergence of the United States as a world golfing leader. Starting with Jock Hutchison's controversial Open victory at St Andrews in 1921, the Americans would win eleven out of the next twelve Open Championships. Following six decades of almost unbroken British success, this period can be described as the 'TransAtlantic Years'.

Walter Hagen was among the first to challenge for the British Open title at Deal in 1920. By the time he set sail for England he had already won two US Opens and proved himself the best player in America. Confidently looking forward to adding the British Open Crown to his collection of titles, Hagen's game was blown away by the high coastal winds of Deal. Unable to match the rapid-fire golf of George Duncan, the eventual winner, Hagen finished in a dismal 53rd position. To his credit, Hagen vowed after the tournament to come back and win – something he would do four times over the next nine years.

The second Open Championship of the immediate post-war period was played at St Andrews in 1921. Apart from the controversy it caused, it was a significant tournament for a number of reasons. Ushering in the end of an era, it was the last occasion where all three members of the Great Triumvirate competed in an Open Championship together. The competition also saw the British Open debut of the player who would come to dominate world golf in the latter half of the 1920s – Bobby Jones.

After his victory at Deal the previous year, George Duncan was favorite to make it an Open double at St Andrews. Duncan, who had entitled his autobiography *Golf at the Gallop*, started well, but fell away badly in the middle rounds. Instead, two other players had tied for first place on 296 – American professional Jock Hutchison and English Amateur Champion Roger Wethered. In those days, the Open Championship was completed in three days, having been increased from two in 1904. The 36-hole play-off was set for the following day – Sunday – but as golf was still not played on the Sabbath in Scotland, it was postponed to the following Monday.

A large crowd gathered to watch the elegant style of the Englishman take on the short, quick-swinging American. The Old Course itself had proved a daunting test all week. With greens baked hard by the combination of an unusually hot summer and drying Scottish wind, many of the world's top golfers had failed to come to terms with it.

The play-off was dominated by Jock Hutchison. Born in St

*Left: Walter Hagen on his way to winning the 1929 Open Championship at Muirfield, Scotland. The most flamboyant golfer of his time, it was not unusual for the 'Haig' to arrive for tournaments in a limousine with a chauffeur and footman.*

*Below: Ribbed-faced irons were specifically designed to impart more back-spin. Later declared illegal by the Rules Committee of the Royal & Ancient, they were used by Jock Hutchison to win his only Open Championship title at St Andrews in 1921.*

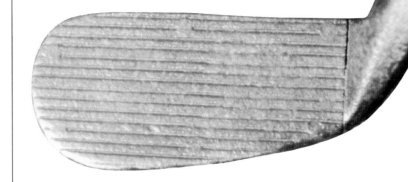

Andrews, Hutchison had moved to Chicago soon after and was now a naturalized American. In his opening round of 72, Hutchison had scored only the second hole-in-one in Open history with his ace on St Andrews par-3 eighth. Throughout the Championship he had amazed everyone with his uncanny ability to hold his iron shots on the rock-hard greens. Repeating the performance in the play-off, he beat Roger Wethered by eight clear strokes to win his one and only Open Championship.

Hutchison openly admitted that his victory was due to the set of deep-grooved 'Bakspin' irons he had had especially made for the Open. An American design, the iron face was lined with deep groves or ridges which imparted a much greater degree of back-spin, the most obvious advantage being the increased control a professional of Huchison's quality would enjoy when playing on rock-hard greens like those at St Andrews. While the Open trophy headed over the Atlantic for the first time in its 61-year history, a major row erupted about the fairness of using such clubs.

The Royal and Ancient made it clear that while using such clubs was not cheating, it was certainly against the spirit of the game. Deep-grooved irons were subsequently banned in Britain and America. Jock Hutchison, who had also triumphed in the United States PGA tournament in 1920, returned to defend his title at Sandwich the following year. He finished well down the field, the Championship was won by Walter Hagen.

Hagen, who had finished sixth at St Andrews, had practiced hard with links golf since his humiliation at Deal two years before. Averaging 75 strokes per round, his score was nothing special but it was enough to edge out British favorite George Duncan and American Jim Barnes. At Hoylake in 1924, Hagen beat Ernie Whitcombe into second place to win his second Open Championship in three years. Still only thirty, he was close to the peak of his playing abilities. From 1924 onwards, Hagen would win four consecutive United States PGA Championships as well as countless other tournaments in the United States. His domination of the British Open Championship in the 1920s would have been just as complete except for the presence of Bobby Jones.

After his mauling at the hands of the Old Course in 1921, Jones returned stronger and wiser for consecutive Open victories in 1926 and 1927. Then with Jones remaining in the United States to concentrate on his law practice, Hagen pulled off consecutive victories of his own at Sandwich in 1928 and Muirfield in 1929. With Hagen and Jones leading the way with seven Open titles between them from 1922 to 1930, it was an unprecedented period of American dominance. Followed by wins for Jim Barnes at Prestwick in 1925, Tommy Armour at Carnoustie in 1931, Gene Sarazen at Princes in 1932, and Denny Shute at St Andrews in 1933, it was a traumatic time for British golfers.

There was one moment of hope at Troon in 1923 when Englishman Arthur Havers gave the home fans something to cheer when he beat Walter Hagen into second place to win a solitary British victory. Apart from the huge Prestwick crowds which cheered ex-Carnoustie man MacDonald Smith in 1925, no home-grown professional had come close to stopping the nine-year American grip. British golf desperately needed a hero and in 1934 at Sandwich it came in the person of Thomas Henry Cotton.

Below: *Walter Hagen holes out on the final green at Muirfield in the British Open Championship in 1927. Partnered by Henry Cotton, his round of 67 gave him his fourth win in the event and confirmed his dominance of the professional game.*

Inset: *Despite winning the Open Championship in 1923 at Troon, British professional Arthur Havers held down a club position throughout his entire career*

**1** *Royal Doulton china cigarette box, 1930.* **2** *Dunlop promotional papier-mache golfer figure, 1930.* **3** *Copeland Spode china baluster mug, 1930.* **4** *Silver brooch with enameled thistle motif, 1930.* **5** *Silver bar-brooch with amber set thistle, 1930.* **6** *Bury Golf Club foursomes trophy in silver, 1935.* **7** *Various golfing figures as trophies, paperweight and cigarette lighter, 1935.* **8** *Porcelain figurine of young lady golfer, 1930.* **9** *Silver pocket watch, modeled on Dunlop mesh golf ball, Swiss-made, 1935.*

enry Cotton was the finest British player of his generation. A complex and often misunderstood individual, his
single-minded dedication to his craft brought him praise and
criticism almost in equal measure. A passionate advocate of
British golf, his first Open victory at Sandwich in 1934 broke a
ten-year American stranglehold on the competition and opened
the floodgates for future British wins.

Left: *One of the first golf professionals to incorporate a strict fitness regime
into his routine, Henry Cotton was still competing well into his fiftieth year.*
Above: *Respective Ryder Cup captains Walter Hagen (USA) and J. H. Taylor
(UK) shake hands in front of Sam Ryder before the start of the 1933 match at
Southport.*
Opposite page, above: *The 'Dunlop 65', named to commemorate Cotton's
inspired round at Sandwich.*

Unusually for a golf professional in the 1930s, Cotton came from a public school background. His father was a successful businessman in Dulwich, South London, and young Henry enjoyed all the privileges that an upper-middle-class education could bring. Apart from a brief appearance in the British Boys' Championship at fourteen, his amateur career was undistinguished. Against the wishes of his father, he left school at seventeen to become an assistant-professional and quickly developed into the most successful British golfer of his generation.

At St Andrews in 1933, Cotton was one of five players sharing seventh position. Gene Sarazen had played well enough to win, but unlike previous Opens at St Andrews, crowds had been down and the atmosphere more muted than before. Golf had become predictable, and for the first time in history so had the Open Championship.

In the following year, Cotton qualified for the Open with a course record 66 at Sandwich itself, and a 75 at nearby Deal.

In the opening two rounds at Sandwich, Cotton played inspired golf. His scores of 67 and 65 were described by Henry Longhurst as having set a standard not yet equalled in the game's history. Having lowered the professional course record twice in three days, Dunlop commemorated Cotton's incredible round by naming their newest golf ball the 'Dunlop 65'.

With the possibility of a British win, the crowds began to flock toward the Kent coast. With the final two rounds played on the Saturday, Cotton scored a steady 72 to build up an unassailable eleven-stroke lead.

Standing on the first tee for the final round, the start was delayed for fifteen minutes while the stewards attempted to gain control of the crowds. Cotton waited in the hut by the first tee, while friends protected him from chaos outside. Suffering from severe stomach cramps, Cotton finally stood up to hit his opening tee-shot. Badly shaken by the whole affair, his struggling final round of 79 was evidence of his strong will and determination. Cotton had won by five clear shots and had finally broken the American hold on the Open Championship.

Henry Cotton was hailed as the best British golfer since the Great Triumvirate. As for the Triumvirate themselves, they had been at Sandwich all week to watch the young Englishman create history. Cotton had publicly thanked J. H. Taylor and James Braid for their support, but before leaving Sandwich he made one final journey. Harry Vardon had sat near the sixth green during the first two rounds, watching the competitors pass by, but his strength had finally give out and he had had to be confined to bed at a local hotel. Shortly after being presented with the Open trophy, Henry Cotton hurried around to the nearby Guildford Hotel and handed the famous silver claret jug into the arms of Harry Vardon. As Vardon clasped it to his chest, both men wept unashamedly.

Henry Cotton's victory at Sandwich had inspired more British success. The following year at Muirfield, the Open was won by robust English professional Alf Perry. A hard-working golfer, Perry had figured in several previous Championships without ever really looking like winning. Technically, Alf Perry was a long way behind many of the top British players. With a golf swing described as 'agricultural', Perry always played with

Left: *A youthful Henry Cotton in 1928.*

Above: *Alf Padgham, the third Englishman to win the Open title in succession with his victory at Hoylake in 1936.*

determination and a great deal of courage, and certainly deserved his one-off victory.

Alf Padgham made it three British victories in succession at Hoylake. According to Henry Cotton, perfect putting had won the Open for the Englishman. Certainly, Padgham had his own unique style which involved standing very upright at the ball with arms pushed out away from his body. It obviously worked because, after becoming *News of the World* Champion in 1930, he had gone on to become a regular tournament winner in Britain. Apart from being a fine putter, Padgham was also renowned for his wonderfully calm temperament on the golf course, one which never wavered during his intense battle with Jimmy Adams during the final round. With Adams in contention right up to the 72nd green Padgham calmly holed out for victory and his first Open title.

The next two Championships were marred by dreadful weather, starting with Cotton's second win at Carnoustie in 1937 and Reg Whitcombe's win at Sandwich in 1938. Carnoustie was one of the longest Open venues at 7,000 yards, and was made considerably longer by the consistent downpours during the final two rounds. With the greens having constantly to be cleared of surface water, the Championship was in danger of not being completed for the first time in its history. Despite the American presence being much stronger than it had been in recent years due to the visiting US Ryder Cup team, Henry Cotton splashed his way to a final 71 for victory.

For Cotton, beating the Americans at Carnoustie was an even more satisfying triumph than winning in 1934. Throughout the Depression years of the 1930s, top American stars like Sam Parks, Ralph Guldahl and Olin Dutra, had consistently stayed away from the Open Championship. With transport not being what it is today, and with better prize money available on the fledgling United States Men's Tour, the Open was deemed low priority by most American professionals.

Britain's golfers saw very little of the great American players who were emerging just before the outbreak of World War II:

Below: *A smiling Henry Cotton after winning the 1937 British Open at Carnoustie.*

Left: *Reg Whitcombe, Open Champion in 1938.*

players like the smooth swinging Sam Snead, Jimmy Demaret, and, greatest of all, the legendary Ben Hogan. Even Byron Nelson who had won the United States Open in 1939, had declined the chance to make it an Open double at St Andrews in the same year. Compared to the austere conditions of British golf where professionals were only just being allowed through the clubhouse doors, the American public treated its golfing stars with adoration. It was understandable therefore, that while these golfing greats were beginning to establish themselves as tournament winners in the late 1930s, they showed little inclination to play in the Open Championship in the United Kingdom.

With little American opposition, Reg Whitcombe continued the British domination of the Open Championship in 1938. Played at Sandwich in gale-force winds, Whitcombe simply controlled the ball better than anyone else. Henry Cotton made a late charge with a 74 in the teeth of the gale, but could only finish third behind perpetual runner-up Jimmy Adams.

The last pre-war Open Championship was played at St Andrews and was won by the tall, big hitting Englishman, Richard Burton. Standing well over 6 feet, Burton had a long, looping swing which enabled him to hit the ball huge distances.

Among the pre-tournament favorites was a talented young Irish amateur called Jimmy Bruen. It was Bruen with his strange, individualistic golf swing that had led the qualifying round with 69 over both the Old and New Courses. With the ever-present threat of the Irishman in his mind, Burton started with 70 and 72 to lead Bruen by five strokes. Then after Bruen blew up with a 77 in the third round, a relieved Dick Burton commented, 'Thank God for that!'

Above: *Dick Burton, Open Champion in 1939 at St Andrews, never recaptured his old form when the championship resumed again in 1946.*

Coming to the 'Home hole' at St Andrews, Burton only needed to par the hole to win. After hitting an enormous drive almost into the Valley of Sin, he casually picked out his wide-sole 'blaster' and flicked the ball up to five feet. Standing on the most famous green in golf, he stroked the putt home and before it had even dropped in the hole, Burton had thrown his putter to the caddy. It brought to a fitting end six years of British domination of the oldest Championship in golf.

There would be other British winners in the decades to come, including a third victory for Henry Cotton in 1948 at Muirfield. But golf, like everything else, had changed. By the time golf resumed again in 1945, not only would new names appear on the Open trophy, but new nationalities: Australians, New Zealanders, South Africans, Argentinians. Golf popularity had spread throughout the world and would remain forever the game of the people.

## Bibliography

ALLISS, Peter, with Michael Hobbs. *The Open.* Collins, London. 1984.

BRAID, James. *Advanced Golf.* Methuen, London. 1908.

BROWNING, Robert. *History of Golf: The Royal and Ancient Game.* Dent, London. 1955.

CLAPCOTT, C. B. *Rules of the Ten Oldest Golf Clubs: 1754 to 1848.* Edinburgh. 1935.

CLAPCOTT, C. B. *The Honourable Company of Edinburgh Golfers on Leith Links: 1744 to 1836.* Privately published. 1939.

CLAPCOTT, C. B. *Some Comments on the Articles and Laws in Playing the Golf.* Privately published. 1945.

CLARK, Robert. *Golf: A Royal and Ancient Game.* Edinburgh. 1875.

COLLETT, Glenna. *Ladies in the Rough.* Knopf, New York. 1928.

DARWIN, Bernard. *Golf Courses of the British Isles.* Duckworth, London. 1910.

DARWIN, Bernard. *A History of Golf in Britain.* Cassell, London. 1952.

EVERARD, H. S. C. *History of the Royal and Ancient Golf Club St Andrews from 1754 to 1900.* William Blackwood, Edinburgh. 1907.

FORGAN, Robert. *The Golfers' Handbook.* John Menzies, London. 1891.

GEDDES, Olive M. *A Swing Through Time: Golf in Scotland 1457–1743.* The National Library of Scotland. HMSO, Edinburgh. 1992.

GOODBAN, J. W. D. *The Royal North Devon Golf Club.* Privately published. 1964.

GRAFFIS, Herb. *The Official History of the Professional Golfers Association of America.* Thomas Y. Crowell, New York. 1975.

HENDERSON, Ian and STIRK, David. *Golf in the Making.* Henderson and Stirk, Winchester. 1979.

HENDERSON, Ian and STIRK, David. *Royal Blackheath.* Henderson and Stirk, Winchester. 1981.

HENGEL, Steven van. *Early Golf: History and Development.* Van Eck, Vaduz. 1972.

HEZLET, May. *Ladies Golf.* Hutchinson, London. 1904.

HOWELL, Audrey. *Harry Vardon: The Revealing Story of a Champion Golfer.* Stanley Paul, London. 1991.

HUTCHINSON, Horace *et al. Golf.* The Badminton Library, Longmans, Green, London. 1890.

HUTCHINSON, Horace. 'Fifty Years of Golf'. *Country Life.* 1919.

JONES, Robert T. *Down the Fairway.* Blue Ribbon Books, New York. 1927.

KEELER, O. B. *The Bobby Jones Story.* Tupper and Love, Atlanta. 1959.

KERR, John. *The Golf Book of East Lothian.* Constable, Edinburgh. 1896.

KIRKALDY, A. *Fifty Years of Golf: My Memories.* Fischer Unwin, 1921.

MacDONALD, Charles Blair. *Scotland's Gift: Golf.* Scribners, New York. 1928.

MacKENZIE, Alister. *Dr. MacKenzie's Golf Architecture.* Simpkin, Marshall, Hamilton and Kent, London. 1920.

McPHERSON, J. Gordon. *Golf and Golfers: Past and Present.* William Blackwood, Edinburgh. 1891.

MARSHALL, J. S. *Old Leith at Leisure.* Edina Press, Edinburgh. 1976.

MARTIN, John S. *The Curious History of the Golf Ball: Man's Most Fascinating Sphere.* Horizon Press, New York, 1968.

MILLER, T. D. *History of the Royal Perth Golfing Society.* Munro Press, Edinburgh. 1935.

MURDOCH, Joseph S. F. *The Library of Golf 1743 to 1966.* Detroit. 1966.

OLMAN, Morton W. and John M. *Golf Antiques and Other Treasures of the Game.* Market Street Press, Cincinnati, Ohio. 1992.

OUIMET, Francis. *A Game of Golf: A Book of Reminiscences.* Houghton Mifflin, New York. 1932.

POTTINGER, G. *Muirfield and the Honourable Company.* Scottish Academic Press, Edinburgh. 1972.

ROBB, George. *Historical Gossip about Golf and Golfers.* Edinburgh. 1863.

ROBBIE, J. Cameron. *The Chronicle of the Royal Burgess Golfing Society of Edinburgh 1735–1935.* Morrison and Gibbs, Edinburgh, 1936.

SALMOND, J. B. *The Story of the R & A.* Macmillan, London. 1956.

SIMPSON, Sir Walter. *The Art of Golf.* Hamilton, Edinburgh. 1887.

SIMPSON, Sir Walter. *The Art of Putting.* Douglas, Edinburgh.1887.

SMITH, Garden G. *The World of Golf.* Isthmian Library, Innes. 1898.

TAYLOR, J. H. *On Golf: Impressions, Comments and Hints.* Methuen, London. 1905.

TULLOCH, W. W. *The Life of Tom Morris.* T. Warner Laurie, London. 1908.

VARDON, Harry. *The Complete Golfer.* Methuen, London. 1905.

WARREN WIND, Herbert. *The Story of American Golf.* Farrar Straus, New York. 1948.

WOOD, Harry B. *Golfing Curios and the Like.* Sherratt and Hughes, London. 1910.

# INDEX

## PICTURE CREDITS

The Publishers would like to thank the photo agencies and photographers who have supplied photographs for this book. The photographs are credited by page number and position on the page as follows: (T) Top; (B) Bottom; (L) Left; (R) Right etc.

The Publishers have endeavoured to ensure that all the photographs in this book are correctly credited. Should any illustration in this book be incorrectly attributed, the Publishers apologize.

Phillips, Chester: Half-title page, contents page, 20-21, 44-45, 66-67 (items 2-14), 94-95, 108-109, 114-115, 136-137.

Royal Collection Enterprises: 14.

Dale Concannon Collection: 13, 36, 38, 39, 42, 43, 49(B), 58(T), 59, 60, 61(B), 61(inset), 62(B), 69, 70, 71, 76(L), 76(R), 78(T), 80(T), 82(T), 82(B), 83, 87(TR), 88(near L), 90, 92(T), 98, 113, 118, 119, 120, 121(T), 121(B), 122(B), 123, 124, 126(BL), 135.

Michael Hobbs Collection: Front and back endpapers, 2, 8-9, 10(T), 10(B), 11, 12, 15, 16, 17(T), 17(B), 18, 19, 22, 22(inset), 23, 24, 25, 26-27, 28(L), 28(R), 29, 30(L), 30(R), 31, 32(T), 32(B), 33(T), 33(B), 34, 35, 37(R), 40, 41, 46(T), 46(B), 47, 48, 49(T), 50, 51, 52-53, 54(T), 54(B), 55(T), 55(B), 56, 57, 58(B), 61(T), 62(T), 63, 63(inset), 65, 66(item 1), 68, 72(L), 72(R), 73(R), 74, 75, 77(T), 77(B), 78(B), 79, 80(B), 84, 85, 85(inset), 86(T), 86(BL), 86(BR), 87(TL), 87(B), 88(far L), 89, 91, 92(B), 93(T), 93(B), 96, 97, 99(T), 99(B), 100, 101, 102(TL), 102(TR), 102(BR), 103, 103(B), 104(T), 104(B), 105, 106, 107(L), 107(R), 110, 111(T), 111(B), 112(T), 112(B), 116, 117(L), 117(R), 122(T), 125(T), 125(B), 125-126, 126, 128, 129, 130, 131, 132, 133, 135(inset), 138(L), 138(R), 139(B), 140(T), 140(B), 141(L), 141(R).